VISIONARY WOMEN

✦

FLORENCE NIGHTINGALE:
LETTERS AND REFLECTIONS

VISIONARY WOMEN

Also in this series:

THE MARTYRDOM OF PERPETUA
Sara Maitland

THE TRIAL OF JOAN OF ARC
Marina Warner

Other titles in preparation

VISIONARY WOMEN

Series editor: Monica Furlong

FLORENCE
NIGHTINGALE

✦

LETTERS AND
REFLECTIONS

with an introduction by
ROSEMARY HARTILL

ARTHUR JAMES

EVESHAM

First published in Great Britain in 1996 by

ARTHUR JAMES LTD
4 Broadway Road
Evesham
Worcestershire WR11 6BH

ISBN 0 85305 353 7

Typeset in Monotype Sabon by
Strathmore Publishing Services, London N7

Printed and bound in Great Britain by
Guernsey Press Ltd, Guernsey, C.I.

Contents

Series Foreword

Women, in our view, have always had interesting and valuable things to say about religious meaning, and about the life of the spirit, often with a different emphasis and accent from men writing and speaking about the same thing. It is not, probably, that women are so very unlike men. It is more that, historically, their life experience has been so different that, as you might expect, they saw events and ideas through a very different glass.

In the case of Christianity it is very difficult to know what they *did* see and feel. For the first eleven centuries of the Christian Church they were almost completely silent, so far as writing and public speaking were concerned, forced to be so partly by lack of education, partly by those deadly chapters in the Epistles that commanded women to be 'silent in the churches', a prohibition that extended beyond the church in a framework that set up rigid conventions, confining women within home or convent. Very, very occasionally a woman's voice breaks through – as Perpetua tells us of the horror of her imprisonment before her martyrdom (third century), or the nun Egeria tells us of her travels (fourth century). It was only from the twelfth century onwards that voices of Christian women began, very tentatively, to emerge, or at least this was the time when women's writings began to be preserved so that they have come down to us.

Nor were other religions so very different. In widely

different cultures and religions – Judaism, Buddhism, Hinduism, Islam – it was assumed, as it was in Christianity, that caring for their husbands and bearing children somehow removed women from making any other sense of their lives or of the world about them. Of course women tried to do it – how can any human being not? – but their views were not sought or recorded.

As a Christian I cannot speak for other religions (though I hope others will speak for some of them in the course of the series), but I observe that everywhere women seem less and less willing to be silent and passive participants. Within Christianity now, there is a healthy and growing remorse for all that was lost when women's voices were silenced.

This series of books attempts to salvage some of the texts (often very little known even by feminists) which remind us what it sounded like when women first began to make their voices heard, and what they said as they described the experiences which shaped their thinking. It also uses material by later women who, one way or an-other, broke new ground in their actions, their ideas and their self-expression. Some of these are well known, but have often been presented to us in oddly distorted ways, which suggests that it is time for some reassessments.

It is not our intention to use these texts wholly uncritically – that would be to patronize the writers – but rather to use them to develop our own thinking. The early material, in particular, often needs effort, as it invites us to make use of ideas, and a view of religion, extraordinarily different from our own.

Our hope is that readers will want to make a small

collection or library of these precious texts – a reparation to the forgotten women, but also, we believe, a fruitful source of inspiration and ideas for ourselves, the fortunate heirs of their courage and determination.

MONICA FURLONG

Acknowledgements

Thanks to Alex Attewell of the Nightingale Museum at St Thomas's Hospital, for access to its collection of Nightingale memorabilia; to Radcliffe and Co., administrators for the trustees of the Henry Bonham Carter Will Trust, for permission to publish extracts from letters now held at the British Library; to the Presbytery of St Mary of the Angels, Bayswater, to quote from a letter to Manning; to the University of Pennsylvania Press for providing accessible material from *Suggestions for Thought*. Other letters and private notes are quoted from various biographies.

Introduction

Florence Nightingale was a religious visionary, rebel and radical. She regarded Christ's whole life as a war upon the restraints of the family; she was highly critical of the Church of England and what she saw as the lukewarm, hypocritical, unthinking religion of much of Victorian England; she was deeply aware of the failures of the church and the growing tide of atheism and indifferentism among working people, disillusioned with conventional religion. Yet her image as the 'Lady of the Lamp' became over the years sentimentalized and sanitized into a pillar of conventional Victorian respectability – a dream model of feminine gentleness, a woman soothing the fevered brow of men.

There are good reasons why she became such a heroine of the English imagination. She transformed the care of wounded and dying soldiers in the Crimean War and founded British modern nursing; she also pioneered modern statistics and the use of the graph, and reformed various aspects of hospital management and construction and British and Indian Army medical administration. But as the fashion for heroines and authoritarian style has declined, her reputation began to lose its brilliance.

Yet more than a hundred years after her work in the Scutari hospital in the 1850s, my Shropshire grammar school was still naming one of its four 'houses' after her and holding her up as an eminent and enlightened woman, a model of sheer bravery and brilliance for the girls to emulate. So her name would ring round the school hall, should her house come first in good conduct, or music, or any of the other competitions the school fostered. We knew she had done wonders in the Crimean War, and of course it was assumed she was a model of Victorian Christian rectitude, dedicated to upholding the Ten Commandments and other biblical virtues.

In fact, when she drew up suggestions for what she considered a more practical religion, she cast a questioning eye on a whole series of traditional religious doctrines and shibboleths: 'The Ten Commandments – are they not full of mistakes?', she wrote. 'The fifth Commandment ("honour your father and your mother, that your days may be long in the land which the Lord your God gives you") contains three mistakes. First, we can only honour that which is honourable; secondly, filial piety has nothing to do with living to old age; thirdly, the Lord did not give them that land (in the sense in which Moses said it) – they took it.' 'There is hardly anything', she sums up trenchantly, 'which it has ever been supposed that God did say, than which we could not have said something better ourselves.'

Yet Florence Nightingale was never a mere iconoclast. She experienced several visions, which she believed came from God; was deeply drawn to the mystics; and she dedicated her life to her ideal of God as perfect wisdom. She regarded her critical questioning as part of her passionate commitment to the search for truth, and for practical action to build the kingdom of heaven on earth. She once remarked to her friend and suitor, Richard Monckton Miles, 'It will never do unless we have a Church of which the terms of membership shall be works, not doctrines.'

Her most lengthy exploration of her religious and philosophical ideas came in a 829-page, three-volume work called *Suggestions for Thought to the Searchers after Truth among the Artizans of England*. It was written to try and encourage new thinking about a sensible, inspiring religion suitable for a scientific age. Drafted before she went to the Crimea, she polished it after her return and in 1860 circulated a few copies among friends.

Extracts from this material, together with other key writings on spiritual and religious matters, are drawn together for the first time in this collection. They reveal a woman struggling with spiritual loneliness, sometimes angry at the mess she feels the church has made of religion, and trying to suggest some answers to the kind of questions about prayer, miracles and how God works on the earth, which still disturb many of us today.

So how much of a force was religion in Florence Nightingale's life? What were her visions like? Why did she become so alienated from conventional religion? What kind of religious conflicts did she face? And how did her religious beliefs change?

Early Life

Florence Nightingale was born in 1820, in the Italian city of Florence, after which she was named. Her family was wealthy, well-to-do, well connected.

The family relationships were complex. Her mother was a powerful personality, whose will came into sharp conflict with her daughter's unconventional, but overwhelming, psychological and personal need to devote her life to the care of the sick. The earliest thing that exists in her daughter's handwriting is said to be a copy of a prescription. Mrs Nightingale found it inconceivable that a daughter of hers should stoop to a job linked almost entirely to disreputable women and disgusting conditions.

Florence Nightingale's father was a relatively weaker character. The third person in the immediate family group was a sibling rival, a bright sister, who was less impressed with Florence and her theories than were some of the many family friends. Before Florence went out to the Crimea, Parthenope thought that Florence made a shocking nurse.

Just before the age of seventeen, Florence had a religious experience which biographers have likened, possibly a shade over-enthusiastically, to the call of Joan of Arc. She described this vision in a private note written thirty years later. Diary: 'On Feb 7th 1837, God spoke to me and called me to His Service.' It appears to have been not an inward revelation, but an 'objective' voice outside herself, speaking in human words.

But a sense of inner guidance had also been experienced far earlier: 'The thoughts and feelings that I have now I can remember since I was six years old ... The first thought I can remember, and the last, was nursing work.' It took until she was in her early thirties to discover exactly what form her call would take and what her mission was to be.

Later, in a private note in 1874, she said voices spoke to her: in 1853 before going to her first position as superintendent at a private hospital for poor gentlewomen in Harley Street; once before her departure to the Crimea in 1855; and once after the death in 1861 of her great friend and collaborator, Lord Sidney Herbert, who was Secretary-at-War in the Crimean period. All occurred, points out Donald Allen, one commentator, after intense emotional and psychological stress marked by personal disappointment, self-doubt and depression, and a sense of failure. All were followed by a strong desire to accomplish something.

The family's religious background was Unitarian but her mother, quite early on, had shifted towards the Church of England, possibly for social reasons. Unitarians – a much more powerful influence in nineteenth-century England than today – rejected the doctrines of the Trinity and Atonement, and combined a strong love for the figure of Jesus with an optimistic attitude to human beings. (In the eighteenth century, many Unitarians had also been radical in politics.) During Florence's lifetime, a new school of Unitarianism developed, which rejected claims of supernatural miracles and interpreted the radical new wave of German historical biblical criticism as throwing doubt on the authority of the Gospels. Florence's own spiritual beliefs, as expressed later in *Suggestions for Thought*, her most extensive piece of writing on religious matters, show strong influence from Unitarian thought. As a youngster, she discussed religious speculation and philosophical ideas with her father.

The American writer, Mrs Julia Ward Howe, who wrote *The Battle Hymn of the Republic*, 'Mine Eyes Have Seen the Glory of the Coming of the Lord', stayed at Embley, one of the family homes, when Florence was about nineteen: 'Florence was elegant rather than beautiful; she was tall and graceful of figure, her countenance mobile and expressive, her conversation most interesting.' Some years later, the novelist, Mrs Gaskell, wrote: 'She is

tall: very straight and willowy in figure; thick and short-
ish rich brown hair; very delicate complexion; grey eyes,
which are generally pensive and drooping, but when they
choose can be the merriest eyes I ever saw; and perfect
teeth making her smile the sweetest I ever saw.'

But by this time Florence had come to regard family
life and its social obligations as a form of tyranny.
Passages in *Suggestions for Thought* which deal with family life give a vivid account of the frustrations of an intel-
ligent young woman, trapped in the round of home and
family life, with no possibility of escape except by marriage into a similar trap:

> What are the thoughts of young girls, while one is singing
> Schubert, another is reading the *Review* and a third is busy
> embroidering? Is not one fancying herself the nurse of some
> new friend in sickness; another engaging in romantic dan-
> gers with him ... another undergoing unheard of trials
> under the observation of someone whom she has chosen as
> the companion of her dream; another having a loving and
> loved companion in the life she's living, which many do not
> want to change?

Many young women, she continues, struggle against this
dreaming as a snare:

> We fast mentally, scourge ourselves morally, use the intel-
> lectual hair-shirt in order to subdue that perpetual day-
> dreaming, which is so dangerous. We resolve 'this day
> month, I will be free from it'; twice a day with prayer and
> written record of the times when we have indulged it, we
> endeavour to combat it. Never with the slightest success. By
> mortifying vanity, we do ourselves no good. It is the want of
> interest in our life, which produces it.

In a private note of 1843, she suddenly realized the disturbing extent to which she was addicted to dreaming. It seems she fell into 'trance-like' states in the midst of ordinary life, like making conversation with social acquaintances at dinner. 'She could not control herself,' says Cecil Woodham-Smith, one of her biographers, 'and gave way with all the shameful ecstacy of the drug-taker.'

For some six years, from the end of 1846 to sometime in 1851, Florence Nightingale lived largely in what Elspeth Huxley calls 'a hell of her own making'. Overwhelmed at times by a sense of guilt, she believed God was punishing her for her unworthiness to do his work: 'No one has had such advantages, and I have sinned with all these. No one has so grieved the Holy Spirit.' A distinct lack of a sense of proportion is evident. Another side of this religiosity was that she imagined herself a victim of special persecution.

One profound influence in her early twenties was her friendship with a relative by marriage known as Aunt Hannah Nicholson, a pure, gentle and deeply religious woman, whose mystical sense of the eternal in everyday life possibly influenced Florence's 1846 letter to a friend about the supernatural (p. 42). She and Aunt Hannah discussed the life of the soul and the way to God.

Her mother expected her to marry. But 'passion, intellect, moral activity – these three have never been satisfied in a woman', Florence Nightingale once wrote. When, in the summer of 1849, after seven years of waiting, she turned down her suitor Richard Monckton Milnes, she commented that she would have found with him intellectual and passionate satisfaction, but the social restraint of a wife's position would have denied her moral satisfaction.

In November 1849, she set off for Egypt with some friends on what turned out to an extraordinary and life-changing journey. She recorded that Christ appeared to her on five occasions, two on successive days. On the way back down the Nile, at Karnak in March 1850, as she sat on the steps of the portico, God spoke to her and 'asked me would I do good for Him alone without the reputation?' At each apparition, she heard him ask the same personal question. Here is a woman all too aware of her ambitious nature, trying to reconcile a strong ego with a loving response to the figure of Christ.

At Thebes, 'as I sat in the large dull room waiting for the letters, God told me what a privilege he had reserved for me ... and how I had been blind to it. If I were never thinking of the reputation, how I should be better able to see what God intends for me.'

Later, in her cabin, alone, she 'settled the question with God', and for about a fortnight was undisturbed by her 'great enemy', dreaming. It was a temporary respite only.

Transition
12 May 1850: 'Today I am 30 – the age Christ began his mission. Now no more childish things. No more love. No more marriage. Now, Lord, let me think only of Thy Will, what thou willest me to do. Oh Lord, Thy Will, Thy Will.'

About four years earlier, the daughter of the Prussian ambassador, friends of the Nightingales, had shown Florence the annual report of Kaiserswerth, a place that had a profound effect on Florence's life. It was a refuge for discharged prisoners in Germany, which had grown also into a school, an orphanage and a hospital. To do the everyday work, an old church order of deaconesses had been revived.

Florence longed to join them, and train there. On 31 July 1850, after considerable opposition from her family, Florence finally managed to visit Kaiserswerth: 'My first night in my own little room within the Anstalt. I felt queer – but the courage, which falls into my shoes in a London drawing room, rises on an occasion like this. I felt so sure it was God's work!' She left a fortnight later 'feeling so brave as if nothing could ever vex me again!' But on her return home there was a huge family row. That year her father was ill.

At the end of the year, ever more frustrated at her family's opposition to her longings to be a nurse, she was writing dark notes:

> I have no desire now, but to die. There is not a night that I do not lie down in my bed, wishing that I may leave it no more ... my present life is suicide. Slowly I have opened my eyes to the fact that I cannot now deliver myself from the habit of dreaming, which, like gin-drinking, is eating out my vital strength. Now I have let myself go entirely. I have no desire but to die.

The social expectations were worse than ever: 'Oh weary days, oh evenings that seem never to end – for how many long years I have watched that drawing-room clock and thought it would never reach the ten, and for twenty or more years to do this.' An undated note, probably from the following year, reveals the same terrible pain: 'Why, oh my God, cannot I be satisfied with the life which satisfies so many people?'

In July 1851, she managed to get herself back to

Kaiserswerth. 'Never have I met with a higher tone, a purer devotion than there.' She later called it her spiritual home. Her mother and sister meanwhile were staying in a comfortable hotel in Carlsbad. In a letter to them, she described her own rather more spartan regime:

> We have ten minutes for each of our meals, of which we have four. We get up at 5; breakfast ¼ before 6. The patients dine at 11, the Sisters at 12. We drink tea (ie a drink made of ground rye) between 2 and 3 and sup at 7. We have two ryes and two broths – ryes at 6 and 3, broths at 12 and 7; bread at the two former, vegetables at 12. ... The world here fills my life with interest and strengthens me in body and in mind.

Here Florence began her nursing training, though she considered the hospital work the least good part of the Institution.

Religion continued to absorb her. Increasingly aware of the failures of the Victorian religious establishment, social religion in England by now had come to seem to her weak and hypocritical. Much orthodox religion struck her as self-absorbed cant. 'Is there anything higher in thinking of one's own salvation than in thinking of one's own dinner?' she once wrote. Her contact with tailors and other working people introduced to her by a friend with a social conscience had shown her how growing numbers of working people were becoming alienated from the church, and turning to atheism or indifference. According to the 1851 census of religion, church attendance in the big industrial manufacturing areas had shrunk to less than a quarter of the population.

That same year, back home from Germany, she jotted down a resolution to devote part of her life to devising 'a new religion for the tailors'. As if that weren't enough, she thought she might also translate the prophets: 'If you could carry out these objects they would keep you healthy. Why can't you get up in the morning? I have nothing I like so much as unconsciousness, but I will try.' The draft for the 'new religion' was eventually to become *Suggestions for Thought*.

Meanwhile, the search for further training continued. In 1852 she wrote to her friend Dr Manning, who had joined the Roman Catholic Church the previous year, and asked him if he could get her into the hospital in Dublin run by the Sisters of Mercy, a nursing order founded some twenty years previously which was doing superb work among the poor. She confessed to being more interested in learning nursing than going on retreat with the sisters. Only a brief visit was possible. Eventually, at the start of 1853, he obtained permission for her to join the Sisters of Charity in Paris. But still her hopes and plans were obstructed: when her grandmother's health worsened, she had to return home to nurse her; then, when she got back to France, she caught measles. Fortunately Florence did not have the kind of faith that interpreted these as signs from the Lord that she should give up her plans.

Throughout the summer of 1852, she seems to have been in religious turmoil. A note records 7 August as the date on which she was conscious of a call from God to be a 'saviour', one of those who save the race from intellectual, social and moral error, by identifying the laws of God, and acting for the benefit of humankind (see p. 103). But how should this be expressed practically?

By now, she had no hopes of the Church of England, though once she would have given it her head, her heart, her hand. 'She told me to go back to do crochet in my mother's drawing room; or if I were tired of that, to marry and look well at the head of my husband's table. ... She gave me neither work to do for her, nor education for it' (p. 49).

The Catholic orders, in contrast, were offering her work, training, sympathy and help. Should she join the Roman Catholic Church? In 1850, a hierarchy of Roman Catholic bishops was established in England; in addition, a number of influential Anglicans were defecting to Rome at rates many regarded as alarming. Her letters reflect some of England's religious turmoil at this time, as well as her own (p. 46).

By now her radical criticisms of a whole series of traditional doctrines, makes it seem at first astonishing that she would consider Rome. No wonder her friend Dr Manning (later Cardinal Manning) was concerned about a certain 'eclecticism' in her thought.

What she admired about Roman Catholicism was its practicality, its businesslike approach to its organization, to the gifts of some women, and its acceptances of doctrine to their logical conclusions. She was also drawn to Roman Catholic saintliness. Moreover, she longed for a spiritual home. When Manning realized the true nature of her beliefs, he advised her against it. When she realized Rome could not be that home, she wrote in August 1852, 'I have had moments of intense discouragement in my life, but never anything like this.'

Meanwhile, family relationships were still less than entirely supportive. In November 1852, sister Parthenope was writing to a mutual friend:

I believe she has little or none of what is called charity or

Philanthropy, she is ambitious – very, and would like well enough to regenerate the world with a grand *coup de main* or some fine institution, which is a very different thing. Here she has a circle of admirers who cry up everything she does or says as gospel, and I think it will do her much good to be with you, who, though you love and admire her, do not believe in the wisdom of all she says and does *because* SHE says it. I wish she could be brought to see that it is the intellectual part that interests her, not the manual. ... When she nursed me, everything which intellect and kind intention could do were done, but she was a shocking nurse.

At last, in August 1853, at the age of 33, Florence Nightingale was installed as unpaid superintendent of an establishment for the care of sick gentlewomen in London – a small private hospital. Her father allowed her £500 a year.

Almost immediately, religion was a renewed cause of controversy. The ladies' committee wanted only members of the Church of England to be admitted. Florence's attitude was patient and tolerant towards a wide variety of beliefs, judging people not on doctrines but on works. She insisted that any woman who was sick and poor, regardless of faith, could be nursed. Eventually a compromise was hammered out:

So now it is settled and in *print* that we are to take all denominations whatsoever and allow them to be visited by their respective priests and Muftis, provided I will receive (in any case whatsoever that is *not* of the Church of England) the obnoxious animal at the door, take him upstairs myself, remain while he is conferring with his patient, make myself *responsible* that he does not speak to, or look at, *anyone else*, and bring him downstairs again in a noose, and out into the street. And to this I have agreed! And this is in print! Amen.

There are disagreements as to how effective she really was in this post, but two things are immediately obvious – her practicality and her political abilities. She considered a lift essential 'to prevent the nurse becoming a pair of legs', and soon learned how to manipulate the committees to get her own way. In January 1854, she wrote to Aunt Hannah: 'I begin the New Year with more true feeling of a Happy New Year than I ever had in my life.'

Crimea

On 14 October 1854, she was invited by her friend, Lord Sidney Herbert, Secretary-at-War, to take a party of nurses to the Crimea, where death-rates from casualties were appalling. She left England a week later. Sidney Godolphin Osborne, a clergyman and a constant contributor to *The Times*, described the impression she gave:

> Miss Nightingale in appearance, is just what you would expect in any other well-bred woman, who may have seen perhaps rather more than 30 years of life; her manner and countenance are prepossessing, and this without the possession of positive beauty; it is a face not easily forgotten, pleasing in its smile, with an eye betokening great self-possession, and giving when she wishes, a quiet look of firm determination to every feature. Her general demeanour is quiet and rather reserved; still I am much mistaken if she is not gifted with a very lively sense of the ridiculous. ... She

has trained herself to command, and learned the value of conciliation towards others, and constraint over herself.

Before Florence Nightingale's party arrived, Sisters of Charity were already doing good work in the French military hospitals. In Scutari, the huge English military hospital with some four miles of rows of wounded patients, conditions were horrific. She discovered that the mortality rate in the barracks was nearly double the mortality of civilian life. 'You might as well take 1,100 men every year out upon Salisbury Plain, and shoot them,' she said, adding that it had become a joke there to offer a prize to anyone ready to take responsibility.

Details are told graphically elsewhere of how she set up diet kitchens, bought in provisions, organized the washing of patients, the cleaning of the wards, the improvement of the drains, and dealt with military and administrative incompetence and opposition. Through these and other factors, mortality at the military hospital of Scutari dropped from 42 per 100 to 2.2. But her best biographer, Cook, said he was not sure that of all her difficulties in the Crimea, the religious one was not 'the most wearing and worrying'.

She and Herbert had wanted to make the first party of nurses to include representatives of all the leading Christian denominations; but owing to the failure of a Protestant institution to supply nurses hoped for, the Roman Catholics and High Church composed the majority of the 38 women. A sectarian hue and cry was the result, with letters in *The Times*. One Irish clergyman, when asked to which sect Miss Nightingale belonged, said of her, 'She belongs to a sect which, unfortunately, is a very rare one; the sect of the Good Samaritan.' A letter (p. 50) to Herbert describes her contemptuous amusement at the idea of herself as conspirator in a Romish plot.

All was complicated by another party from England, led by Mary Stanley, which included a group of Irish nuns under Mother Frances Bridgman, nicknamed 'Brickbat' by Nightingale, from whom she had refused to take orders:

> The Roman Catholic remains unsettled – Brickbat, the Reverend Mother of Kinsale, refusing to let five of her nurses come here without her to be under our Reverend Mother, thereby showing she has some second view besides Nursing – and I refusing to let our little society become a hotbed of Roman Catholic intriguettes. Of course we shall have a Roman Catholic storm. But *our* Reverend Mother, head and heart with us, is doing her best to stop it.

Nightingale wanted nurses not chaplains; but some of the Roman Catholic nurses were accused of 'proselytizing' among their non-Catholic patients. This was countered by allegations that some of the Protestant nurses neglected their Roman Catholic patients. All this she had to try and sort out.

Meanwhile she carried on with the rest of her work. Osborne said she had an 'utter disregard for contagion. I have known her spend hours over men dying of cholera or fever.' She is also said to have been wonderful at cheering up anyone who was low. Writing later, she herself reckoned that the best way to cheer up a patient was to share news of some success story:

Tell him of a benevolent act which has really succeeded practically – it is like a day's health to him. You have no idea what the craving of the sick, with undiminished power of thinking, but with little power of doing, is to hear of good practical action, when they can no longer partake in it.

What troubled patients, she discovered, were apprehension, uncertainty, waiting, expectation and fear of surprise: '[These] do a patient more harm than any exertion.'

In a letter to the Crimea, her sister Parthenope wrote: 'In spite of it all, have you not found your true home – the home of your spirit?'

Later life

Florence Nightingale returned from the Crimea at thirty-seven with broken health. To begin with, she worked hard submitting material to government commissions involved, among other things, with establishing a military statistical department, creating an army medical school, and improving military barracks, which she regarded as badly lit and ventilated. She always preached the gospel of fresh air. Her goal was the health of the soldiers. 'I stand at the altar of murdered men, and while I live I fight their cause,' she wrote in a private note.

She also redrafted her earlier ideas for *Suggestions for Thought* and in 1860 circulated a few privately printed copies to friends. 'She had set out to give the working classes a religion,' wrote one friend, Madame Mohl, 'and gave them a philosophy instead.' 'There is nothing so exhausting', she once said, 'as a companion who is always *effleurant* [touching lightly] the deeper subject; ... as a person who is always inquiring and never coming to any solution or decision. I don't know whether Hamlet was mad. But certainly he would have driven me mad.'

Her attempt in *Suggestions for Thought* was – even on the vast subject of religion – to try and point the way to some solutions and decisions. She recognized that the essence of God would always remain a mystery, but she believed the character of God was knowable. Similarly, his laws were discoverable by experience, research and analysis. In this she was responding to the Positivists, who argued that the moral world, just as the physical world, was entirely governed by laws. Nightingale's criticism of the Positivists was that they had not taken the world one step beyond that: 'They have not told us what one of those laws is.' She also parted company with the Positivists in believing in a transcendent God, in a life after death, and that all human beings had a divine nature.

Her vision of God is as a figure of Perfect Wisdom and Benevolence – an objective Truth, whose character can be known. God's laws have an eternal sequence of cause and effect. In this ordered universe, miracles have no place. But Florence Nightingale was not a determinist. Instead, she believed men and women are called to be co-creators with God. Their role is to strive for the betterment of others through discovering what these laws are and acting accordingly. In a letter to her friend, Benjamin Jowett, she put it this way: 'It is a religious act to clean out a gutter and to prevent cholera, and it is not a religious act to pray (in the sense of asking).' Suffering occurs when God's laws are ignored; so suffering is a necessary signpost by which human beings come to recognize those laws.

Through observing and identifying these laws, we will evolve towards the kingdom of heaven on earth. Nightingale was an idealist, but nothing if not a practical idealist. In developing these ideas, she casts doubt on the atonement, on miracles, on hell, on the final authority of the Bible, and on traditional ideas of prayer and forgiveness.

It is easy to see why her friends advised her against publication. Criticism of church doctrine by clergy and academics was a sackable offence at this time. When F. D. Maurice expressed doubts about eternal punishment in 1853, he was dismissed from his post at King's College, London. Nightingale could not be dismissed, but the climate was not tolerant.

Given the likely controversy, another problem was the nature of the writing itself. Fundamentally, the work is still just a draft. It includes exaggerations, generalizations, some errors of fact, and at times a flippant tone (though that can make for some entertaining reading). Sometimes it is repetitive and badly organized. In the extracts included in this selection, reordering and reorganizing has been necessary. To help clarity for the modern reader, I have introduced new headings.

Meanwhile, ill health still dogged her since her return, exhausted, from the Crimea. Following a relapse of her illness in 1861, she was bed-ridden for the next six years with severe spinal pain. Some of her biographers have accused her of a form of malingering, as a kind of ruse to get on with her work undisturbed. 'Her indeterminate illness did not give her doctors much to work on,' writes the historian Professor F. B. Smith. 'It remains indisputable that whenever Miss Nightingale announced herself to be ill, she was busy.' In fact, recent evidence indicates Miss Nightingale is owed an apology. Her illness now seems to have been genuine, a cause not only of great physical pain but also profound melancholy. It was probably brucellosis, developed in the Crimea. Caused by contaminated milk, it attacks the nerves and lower back. It can also cause symptoms easily mistaken as psychosomatic – depression, loss of appetite, palpitation and nervous tremors.

In the solitude of her chamber, she worked and worked: founding St Thomas's Medical School, writing on nursing, later working for the Indian Commission. 'I have done nothing for seven years', she said to a friend at one point, 'but write regulations.' But she also wrote spiritual meditations, reams of confessions, self-examination, communings with God.

A large number of her notes and observations on spiritual matters still exist. She wrote them on anything that came to hand – in letters, on bits of blotting paper, on backs of calendars, the margins of letters. Some are dated, some not. They include reflections on Islam, Zoroastrianism, Hinduism, Buddhism and ancient Egyptian religion. A glance at her personal copy of the Bible (now in the possession of the Nightingale Museum at St Thomas's Hospital, London) shows close annotation in no less than six languages: English, German, Greek, Latin, Italian and French.

From 1872, a mood of deep dejection set in. She had tried to apply her religion to every aspect of her life, but her philosophical speculations about law and the character of God did not necessarily help with trials on an everyday level. She found it hardest to obtain patience and resignation. In her eyes, friendship meant 'Devotion to a common purpose in active life and equal zeal in the co-operative prosecution of it'. She found it hard to forgive friends who strayed from her own sense of purpose.

A close friend by now was Benjamin Jowett, later Master of Balliol College, Oxford, and subject of a rhyme, composed in the late 1870s by some college members:

> First come I; my name is Jowett.
> There's no knowledge but I know it.
> I am Master of this college:
> What I don't know isn't knowledge.

At the end of 1872, he asked her to make a selection of Bible stories for a children's Bible. On this too, she had trenchant opinions. Sending her selection, she wrote:

> The story of Achilles and his horses is far more fit for children than that of Balaam and his ass, which is only fit to be told by asses. The stories of Samson and of Jephthah are only fit to be told to bull dogs; and the story of Bathsheba to be told to Bathshebas. Yet we give all these stories to children as 'Holy Writ'.

She summarized the book of Samuel and the books of Kings as 'Witches. Harlots. Talking Asses. Asses Talking. Young Gentlemen caught by the Hair. Savage Tricks. Priests' Tales.' Jowett, says the biographer Woodham-Smith, was delighted, said her suggestions had been adopted almost entirely and that he blessed her every time he took up the book.

In 1873, some reworked fragments of *Suggestions for Thought* were published in two articles in *Fraser's*

Magazine. Thomas Carlyle is reported to have said of the second Fraser article that Miss Nightingale was like 'a lost lamb bleating on a mountain' – a remark she did not relish. Some readers, shocked by her views, wrote to say they would pray daily for her conversion.

Mysticism

That year, Jowett urged her to complete a work she had already begun. It was on medieval mystics. 31 October:

> You will do a good work if you point out the kind of mysticism which is needed at the present day – not mysticism at all, but as intense a feeling as the mystic had of the power of truth the will of God.

To many Victorians and many since, mysticism is apart from ordinary life, something best left to saints in convents and hermits in cells. Florence Nightingale was not a contemplative, but an administrator. Yet she longed for the union of mysticism with a busy and active life.

Jowett wrote on 18 April suggesting she add a preface, explaining her understanding of mysticism and giving guidance as to how mystical books should be used now. He wrote:

> I think it is clear that this mystic state ought to be an occasional and not a permanent feeling – a taste of heaven in daily life. Do you think it would be possible to write a mystical book which would also be the essence of Common Sense?

In notes, Nightingale wrote:

> Religion is not devotion, but work and suffering for the love

of God. This is the true doctrine of Mystics. ... Where shall
I find God? In myself. That's the true Mystical Doctrine. But
then I myself must be in a state for Him to come and dwell
in me. That is the whole aim of the mystical life. (p. 53–4)

But she felt she herself had failed. That became a
source of spiritual torment. 'True religion is to have no
other will but God's,' she quoted from a sixteenth-
century work. She felt she had tried to force her will on
God. She covered bits of paper with gloomy thoughts.
Occasional shafts of her caustic humour break through: 'I
MUST remember God is not my private secretary.'

The work was to be called 'Notes from Devotional
Authors of the Middle Ages collected, chosen and freely
translated by Florence Nightingale'. Among those to be
included was the Spanish sixteenth-century mystic, St
Teresa of Avila, though, certainly earlier in life,
Nightingale had regarded Teresa's god as merely capricious, rather than lawful (pp. 75 and 96). As the years of
her mother's old age and senility dragged on, the work
became a solace, a 'taste of heaven in daily life' as one
biographer puts it.

In so far as she believed in an objective Truth, independent of the human mind, Nightingale was a Platonist.
She thought there were curious analogies between Plato
and the medieval mystics. One of her favourite prayers
was the closing prayer in the Phaedrus: 'Give me beauty in
my inward soul, and may the outward and inward man be
at one.' She thought it unequalled by any collect or the
service book; it 'puts in 17 words the whole, or at least
half the doctrine of St John of the Cross'.

As domestic complications increased, her life, it seems,

became a round of coaxing servants, humouring her parents, struggling to persuade them to straighten their neglected affairs. By December, she wrote to a friend she was 'completely broken'. When her father died in January, she had to sort out the business and take responsibility for her ailing mother. The summer and autumn of 1874 was probably the most unhappy time of her life. Writing now became impossible, and the book on mystics was laid aside, never to be completed.

One night Florence described how the shadow cast by the night-light on the wall reminded her of Scutari: 'Am I she who once stood on that Crimean Height? "The Lady with the Lamp shall stand." The lamp shows me only my utter ship wreck.'

Later in life her melancholy declined, her health improved, and she continued her public work, though she never published anything else on the subject of religion. She considered action much more important than literature; in many ways, she had a profound distrust of writing as a substitute for action. Her last years were peaceful; photographs reveal a benevolent-looking old lady. She died in 1910, at the age of ninety.

No one could doubt her commitment to the God of perfect Wisdom that she described in *Suggestions for Thought*. Yet her biographer, Cook, describes her aim as a 'kingdom of more airy hospitals, more scientific nursing, brighter barracks, cleaner homes, better-laid drains'. The Aga Khan once asked her, as he listened to her tale of sanitary improvements during fifty years of active life, 'But are your people better?'

In the light of the Holocaust in the Second World War,

the 'ethnic cleansing' in former Yugoslavia, and the mass graves of Kampuchea, Florence Nightingale's belief in evolutionary progress, as God's moral laws are more clearly perceived, seems to embody more optimism than we can quite share. But she never thought progress would be easy. Her advice is to listen well to the stories of these horrors: 'It is the Eternal voice – "Not so, my Children."' She heard that same voice repeated in every cholera, massacre, vice and degeneration, and understood it as God's call to each one of us:

> Man usually replies to it by prayer, (if he replies to it at all,) prayer for the removal of the evil. And the Eternal voice answers again, Not so ... Will you betake yourselves to prayers for the salvation of man to Another, whose express plan it is that it shall be your own noble work? The poisoned, the paralysed nature cannot help itself. Man must rise up and save.

Today, the 'Lady with the Lamp' is still the image of Florence Nightingale that haunts the English imagination. And why not? She held high a light of humanity, courage and sheer common sense in the dark face of official apathy, fudge, hypocrisy and irresponsibility. Her goal was to relieve people's sufferings, and she did. By the light of her lamp, she took a long, steady look at what was really before her, marshalled the facts, drew up practical ideas for radical change, and then worked day and night to achieve them through the political process. To do this, she made use of an authority and confidence instilled by her class and the wide range of contacts she had made socially through her family. She also exercised forceful persuasiveness, tenacity, relentless hard work, political nous and gumption. And woe betide any friend who let her down on the way.

Yet the image of the 'Lady with the Lamp' became, in the public imagination, sentimentalized into a dream: a Victorian male fantasy of a gentle, feminine, domestic, presence, moving quietly from bed to bed, stroking a fevered brow, cherishing a wounded hero, murmuring a comforting word – a merging of mother, beloved, angel, and the Virgin Mary.

Of course, it is nonsense. Parthenope, her sister, knew that. She recognized early on that it was the intellectual part of nursing that interested Florence, not the manual. Parthenope also knew in intimate detail of the struggle Florence had waged for years with her family to escape the limitations of that domestic ideal of traditional femininity, and to achieve an independent, autonomous life, where all her remarkable gifts could be freely used. It was that very straitjacket of Victorian female domesticity that had excluded her from university education or other formal training. Certainly her father seems to have educated her and Parthenope remarkably well at home; but that Florence so transcended the inevitable limitations of such an education – pioneering the mathematical use of graphs, designing hospitals, tackling complex philosophical ideas, and so on – is another sign of her brilliance.

The writings collected in this book reveal a real person, rather than just a fantasy – a woman capable of caustic humour, satirical observation, with a gift for words and imagery, intellectually radical and open-minded, and sometimes driven to fury by social and religious hypocrisies.

I think of her now, trying to do God's work, struggling

to recognize the order of the universe, and fighting off a temptation to organize God, and I am proud that my school named one of its houses in her honour.

ROSEMARY HARTILL

Numbers in square brackets, e.g. [4], refer to the Notes which begin on p. 155.

1 Letters and Private Notes

Anglo-Catholic England
September 1841. Letter to Miss Clarke:

We have just returned from the Leeds consecration [of an Anglican bishop], and a more curious or interesting sight I never saw. Imagine a procession of 40 clergymen, all in their white robes, with scarfs of blue and black and fur and even scarlet, so that I thought some of them were cardinals. ...

It was quite a gathering place for Puseyites from all over England. Papa heard them debating, whether they should have lighted candles before the Altar, but they decided no, because the Bishop of Ripon would not like it – however they had them in the evening and the next morning when he was gone – and Dr Hook [vicar of Leeds] has the regular Catholic jerk in making the genuflexion every time he approaches the altar. The church is a most magnificent one, and every one has contributed their best to it, with a true Catholic spirit; one gave the beautiful painted window, another the Correggio for the Altar piece, the Queen Dowager the Altar-cloth, another the bells, etc., etc. ... During the consecration, I wished to have been a clergyman, but when Mrs Gaskell [the novelist] and I came down afterwards for the Sacrament, I could not help looking in the faces of the clergymen, for the impression I expected to see, as they walked down the aisle, and wandered about (this

immense crowd) after the Sacrament – and oh! I was woe-
fully disappointed – they looked so stupid; and I could not
help thinking, If you had been Catholics, you would all have
been on your knees during the service, without minding
your fine gowns and the cold stones.

Temptation

October 1845. Letter to a friend, describing the scene at
the bedside of her favourite little cousin:

One night, when I was ready to share the verse about the
temptation of the world, the flesh and the devil, and we were
agreeing that the temptations of the flesh were liking a great
deal of play and no work, and lying long in bed, and the
temptations of the world liking to be praised and admired,
and be a general favourite; and so on, more than anything
else, and we were both very much affected, he said before I
left him, 'Now I may lie in bed tomorrow, and you won't call
me at six, will you?' And I too went away to dream about a
great many things which I had much better not think about.
Oh, how I did laugh at the results of all our feelings! To
think and to be are two such different things!

The supernatural

August 1846. Letter to Miss Clarke:

I fancy you live much more in the supernatural than the natural world. I always believe Homer; and in St Paul's 'cloud
of witnesses'; and in the old Italian pictures, which have a
first story, where the unseen live *au premier*, with a two pair
back, where the *Père Eternel's* shadow is half seen peeping

out, and a ground floor where poor mortals live, but still have a connection with the Establishment upstairs. I like those books where the Invisible communicates freely with the Visible Kingdom; not that they ever come up to one's idea, which is always so much brighter than the execution (for the word is only the shadow cast by the light of thought); but they are suggestive. I always believe in a multitude of spirits inhabiting the same house with ourselves; we are only the entresol, quite the most insignificant of its lodgers, and too busy with our pursuit of daily bread, too much confined with hard work, and too full of the struggle with the material world, to visit the glorious beings immediately about us – whom we shall see, when the present candle of our earthly reason is put out, which blinds us just as the candle end, left burning after one is in bed, long prevents us from seeing the world without, lit up by the full moon. It trembles and flickers and sinks into its socket, and then we catch a bright stripe of moonlight shining on the floor; but it flares up again, and the silvery stream is gone 'as if it could not be, as if it had not been' and we can see nothing but the candle, and hardly imagine any other light – till at last it goes quite out, and the flood of moonlight rushes into the room and every pane of the casement window, and every ivy leaf without, are stamped, as it were, upon the floor, and a whole world revealed to us, which that flickering candle was the means of concealing from us. This is what Jesus Christ meant, I suppose, when He said He must go away in order to be with his friends in His spirit, that he would be much nearer to them after death than in the flesh. In the flesh we were separated from our friends by their going into the next room only – a door, a partition divided us; but what can separate two souls? ...

What shall we say if, one day, the moon rises upon our spiritual world, and we see close at hand ready to hold the most intimate communion with us, those spirits, whom we had loved and mourned as lost to us? We are like the blind men by the wayside, and ought to sit and cry, Lord, that we may receive our sight! And when we do receive it, we shall perhaps find that we require no transplanting into another world ... what we require is sight, not change of place, I believe.

Fighting against evil
24 September 1846. Letter to Miss Clarke:

I feel my sympathies are with Ignorance and Poverty. ... My imagination is so filled with the misery of this world that the only thing in which to labour brings any return, seems to me helping and sympathizing there; and all that poets sing of the glories of this world appears to me untrue: all the people I see are eaten up with care or poverty or disease. I know that it was God who created the good, and man the evil, which was not the will of God, but the necessary conse-quence of His leaving free-will to man. I know that misery is the alphabet of fire, in which history, with its warning hand, writes in flaming letters the consequences of Evil (the Kingdom of Man), and that without its glaring light we should never see the path back into the Kingdom of God, or heed the directing guide-posts. But the judgments of nature (the law of God) as she goes her mighty, solemn, inflexible march, sweeps sometimes so fearfully over man that though it is the triumph, not the defeat of God's truth and of His laws that falsehood against them must work misery, and misery is here perhaps the strongest proof that His loving hand is present, yet all our powers, hopes and fears must, it seems to me, be engrossed by doing His work for its relief. Life is no holiday game, nor is it a clever book, nor is it a school of instruction, nor a valley of tears; but it is a hard fight, a struggle, a wrestling with the Principle of Evil, hand to hand, foot to foot. Every inch of the way must be disputed. The night is given us to take breath, to pray, to drink deep at the fountain of power. The day, to use the strength which has been given us, to go forth to work with it till the evening. The Kingdom of God is coming; and 'Thy Kingdom Come' does not mean only 'My salvation come'.

Forgiveness
12 October 1848. Letter to her father:

I have often wondered how Christ could teach that prayer, 'And forgive us our trespasses, as we forgive those who trespass against us' – when certainly that is not what we wish but a great deal more. But that prayer, it now seems to me, was the most practical embodying of a great philosophical truth, perhaps the only intelligible popular form of it. For, first we must begin by making the effort to forgive others ourselves, before we can possibly realize that God can extend forgiveness to us. Next, we must have learned to forgive others spontaneously before we can believe in the spontaneous forgiveness of God and what is the next step which takes place in ourselves? Why, we begin to see (after having practised these two long enough) that we have no business with forgiveness, for we had no business to feel the angry revengeful feelings ... the renunciation of feelings in ourselves is what we agreed to call 'forgiveness' and till we see this, see, i.e. that forgiving is giving up an evil passion in ourselves, we cannot realize the great truth, that there is no forgiveness in God – forgiveness being essentially the property of a fallible being, not of God, (tho' the Collect does say so) who has nothing to do with it. This Truth now appears, not as the opposite proposition to Christ's prayer, but as its natural and direct consequence at which indeed we could not have arrived without praying long and often (till it became a practice) that prayer. And as Religion is the popular practical form of Philosophy, – so that prayer Christ saw to be the only practical ladder to this great idea of the nature of God.

The Catholic Church
Notebook 1849:

In all the dens of disgrace and disease, the only clergy who deserve the name of pastors are the Roman Catholics. The rest, of all denominations – Church of England, Church of Scotland, Dissenters – are only theology or tea mongers.

Considering conversion to Roman Catholicism
7 February 1851. Letter to Madame Mohl (formerly Miss Clarke):

I suppose you know how the two Churches have been convulsing themselves in England in a manner discreditable to themselves and ridiculous to others. The Anglican Church screamed and struggled as if they were taking away something of hers, the Catholic Church sang and shouted as if she had conquered England – neither the one nor the other has happened. Only a good many people (in our Church) found out they were Catholics and went to Rome, and a good many other people found out they were Protestants, which they never knew before, and left the Puseyite pen, which has now lost half its sheep. At Oxford, the Puseyite volcano is extinct ...

You know what a row there will be this Session in Parliament about it. The most moderate wish for a Concordat, but even these say we must strip the R. C. Bishops of their new titles. Many think the present Gov. will go out upon it, because they won't do enough to satisfy the awakened prejudices of dear John Bull. I used to think it was a mere selfish quarrel between red stockings and lawn sleeves; but not a bit of it; it's a real popular feeling. One would think that all our religion was political by the way we talk, and so I believe it is. From the rising of the sun to the going down of the same, you hear our clergy talking of nothing but Bishop versus Vicars General – never a word of different plans for education, prisons, penitentiaries, and so on. One would think we were born ready made as to education, but that art made a Church.

I feel little zeal in pulling down one Church or building up another, in making Bishops or unmaking them. If they would make us, our Faith would spring up of itself, and then we shouldn't want either Anglican Church, or R. C. Church, to make it for us. But, bless my soul, people are just as ignorant now of any law in the human mind as they were in Socrates' time. We have learnt the physical laws since then; but mental laws – why, people don't even acknowledge their existence. They talk of grace and divine influence, – why, if it's an arbitrary gift from God, how unkind of Him not to give it before! But people in England think it quite profane to talk of finding them out, and they pray 'That it may please Thee to have mercy upon all men,' when I should knock you down if you were to say to me 'That it should please you to have mercy upon your boy' … I wish everybody would write as far as they can A Short Account of God's Dealings with them, like the old Puritans, and then perhaps we should find out at last what are God's ways in his goings on and what are not.

July 13 1852. Letter to Revd Henry Manning (later Cardinal Manning):

You suspect me of Eclecticism. I do not know, I will think about it. The whole age is invaded by it, and by its offspring Indifferentism. I thought I had as great a horror of it as you had. But one is always wrong about oneself, and therefore I think it most probable you have found me out.

She despised the Church of England, yet could not convert:

The wound is too deep for the Church of England to heal. I belong as little to the Church of England as to that of Rome – or rather my heart belongs as much to the Catholic Church as to that of England – oh, how much more. The only difference is that the former insists peremptorily upon my believing what I cannot believe, while the latter is too careless and indifferent to know whether I believe it or not. She proclaims out of the Prayer Book what we are to believe, but she does not care whether we do (and we don't), while the Catholic Church examines into the fact. If it were not for that, I might have a home where now I have none.

26 November 1852. Letter to Arthur Stanley (later Dean Stanley), who had asked her to help dissuade a friend from becoming a Roman Catholic. She said she remained an Anglican because she was born there, and feared his friend might consider the arguments she could urge against the Roman Catholics applied equally against Anglicans. On the other hand, Roman Catholicism offered advantages to women that the Church of England did not:

> The Catholic orders offered me work, training for that work, sympathy and help in it, such as I had in vain sought in the Church of England. The Church of England has for men bishoprics, archbishoprics and a little work (good men make a great deal for themselves). For women, she has – what? I had no taste for theological discoveries. I would have given her my head, my heart, my hand. She would not have them. She did not know what to do with them. She told me to go back to do crochet in my mother's drawing room; or if I were tired of that, to marry and look well at the head of my husband's table. You may go back to Sunday school, if you like it, she said. But she gave me no training even for that. She gave me neither work to do for her, nor education for it.

Ecumenism

28 January 1855. Letter from the Crimea to Lord Sidney Herbert, Secretary-at-War:

> They tell me that there is a religious war about poor me in *The Times* and that Mrs Herbert has generously defended me. I do not know what I have done to be so dragged before

the Public. But I am so glad that my God is not the God of the High Church or of the Low, that he is not a Romanist or an Anglican – or a Unitarian. I don't believe he is even a Russian, though his events go strangely against us. (NB A Greek once said to me at Salamis, 'I do believe God Almighty is an Englishman'.)

Prayer

Notes of a conversation with Florence Nightingale, made by her friend, the poet A. H. Clough, 2 March 1859:

> The excellence of God, she said, is that He is inexorable. If he were to be changed by people's praying, we should be at the mercy of who prayed to Him. It reminded her, she said, of what old James Martin said some years ago when she saw him – that he didn't like having dissenters praying – he liked to have the prayers all set down and arranged: he didn't know what people mightn't be praying, perhaps that the money might be taken out of his pocket and put into theirs.

Descending into hell – spiritual loneliness

12 July 1865. Letter to Benjamin Jowett:

> You are quite right in what you say of me. I mar the work of God by my impatience and discontent. I lost my serenity some years ago – then I lost clearness of perception, so that sometimes I did not know whether I was doing right or wrong for two minutes together – the horrible loneliness – but I don't mean to waste your time. Only I would say that my life, having been a fever, not even a fitful one, is not my own fault. Neck or nothing has been all my public life. It has

never been in my power to arrange my work. No more than I could help having to receive and provide for four thousand patients in 17 days [in the Crimean War]. ... Then with the intolerable sleeplessness. But instead of that, I think I do worse every day. I do think God 'descending into hell' – whatever that word may mean in the creed – is perfectly true in two senses: that God making his worlds is God descending into hell – and that to do his work does entail upon some people descending into hell. They deteriorate under it. Still it is their fault ...

Mine has been such a horrible loneliness. But many women, maids of all work, and poor governesses, have been much more lonely than I – and have done much better than I ...

I think, if I had felt God loved me, I could have done anything. ... But I never could feel it.

I am even more broken in mind, than in body, though I don't think my mind ever was a strong one.

Yet I believe I am willing to do God's work anyhow and leave all the rest to Him.

Jowett tried to encourage her, reminding her of victories.

9 August 1872. Letter to Jowett:

You tell me to look back on the good that's been done.

I cannot.

It is not in me.

I am just as much stripped of my past life, 'stand naked there' on the brink of the grave, as if it had really been done in another life.

It seems as if I had given away my deeds and could not

feel them back again – or remember to what I had given them.

But I can remember quite and very well my evil deeds ...

I have none and many friends. And I feel inclined to say, And is this all? Can Friendship do [no] more – but ask me to write another letter? which won't be read either?

But I do trust in God
    though not as I should.

Votes for women

11 August 1867. Letter to John Stuart Mill, in which she turned down his request to play a prominent role in the newly formed National Society for Women's Suffrage:

That women should have the suffrage, I think no one can be more deeply convinced than I. ... But it will probably be years before you obtain the suffrage for women. And, in the meantime, are there not evils which press much more hardly on women than not having the vote? ...

Could not the existing disabilities as to property and influence of women be swept away by the legislature as it stands at present? – and equal rights and equal responsibilities be given as they ought to be, to both men and women? I do not like to take up your time giving instances, redressible by legislation, in which women, especially poor married women with children, are most hardly pressed upon now. I have been a matron on a large scale the greater part of my life, and no matron with the smallest care for her nurses can be unaware of what I mean e.g. till a married woman can possess property there can be no love and no justice.

Making heaven on earth
c. 1868. Fragment of a letter, possibly to Jowett:

I entirely repudiate the distinction usually drawn between the man of thought and the man of action, between the seeker of the ideal (philosopher) and the political man ...

I too should be a much happier and better woman, if I were to be *thinking* only of the Ideal, if I were writing about an ideal moral Army – instead of struggling daily, hourly, with the selfishness, indifference, wilful resistance, which are all that surround me now – while you (my Interlocutor) are in the calm regions of the ideal. It is the difference between swimming against a strong current, with the waves closing over your head, (which is my state now) and standing on the bank, looking at the blue sky. ...

No, let the Ideal go, if you are not trying to *incorporate* it in daily life.

Mysticism
c. 1873. Rough draft of notes for the preface of a book about mystics (never completed):

That religion is not devotion, but work and suffering for the love of God; this is the true doctrine of Mystics – as is more particularly set forth in a definition of the sixteenth century: 'True religion is to have no other will but God's.' Compare this with the definition of Religion in Johnson's *Dictionary*: 'Virtue founded upon reverence of God and expectation of future rewards and punishments'; in other words, on respect and self-interest, not love. Imagine the religion which inspired the life of Christ 'founded' on the motives given by Dr Johnson!

Christ himself was the first true Mystic 'My meat is to do the will of Him that sent me and to finish His work ...'

Where shall I find God? In myself. That is the true Mystical Doctrine. But then I myself must be in a state for Him to come and dwell in me. This is the whole aim of the Mystical Life. That the soul herself should be in heaven, that our Father which is in heaven should dwell in her, that there's something within us infinitely more estimable than often comes out, that God enlarges this 'palace of our soul' by degrees so as to enable her to receive Himself, that He gives her liberty but that the soul must give herself up absolutely to Him for Him to do this, the incalculable benefit of this occasional, but frequent intercourse with the Perfect; this is the conclusion and sum of the whole matter, put into beautiful language by the Mystics ...

These old Mystics whom we call superstitious were far before us in their ideas of God and prayer (that is, of our communion with God). 'Prayer', says a mystic of the sixteenth century, 'is not to ask what we wish of God, but what God wishes of us.' [In the prayers of mystics there is scarcely a petition.] There is never a word of the theory that God's dealings with us are to show His 'power'; still less of the theory that 'of His own good pleasure' He has 'predestined' any souls to eternal damnation. There is little mention of heaven for self; of desire for happiness for self, none. It is singular how little mention there is either of 'intercession' or of 'Atonement by another's merits'. True it is that we can only create a heaven for ourselves and others 'by the merits of Another', since it is only by working in accordance with God's Laws that we can do anything. But there is nothing at all in these prayers as if God's anger had to be bought off, as if He had to be bribed into giving us heaven by sufferings merely 'to satisfy God's justice'. In the dying prayers, there is nothing of the egotism of death. It is the reformation of God's church – that is, God's children, for whom the self would give itself – that occupies the dying thoughts. There is not often a desire to be released from trouble and suffering. On the contrary, there is often a desire to suffer the greatest suffering, and to offer the greatest offering, with even greater pain, if so any work can be done. And still, this, and all this, is ascribed to God's *goodness*! ...

The way to live with God is to live with Ideas – not merely to think about ideals, but to do and suffer for them. Those who have to work on men and women must above all have their Spiritual Ideal, their purpose, ever present. The 'mystical' state is the essence of common sense.

Notes on Catherine of Siena:

It is not the occupation, but the spirit that makes the difference. The election of a bishop may be a most secular thing. The election of a representative may be a religious thing. It is not the preluding such an election with public prayer that would make it a religious act. It is religious so far as each man discharges his part as a duty and a solemn responsibility. The question is not whether a thing is done for the State or the Church, but whether it is done with God or without God.

1889. Letter to Jowett:

For myself the mystical and spiritual religion as laid down by St John's gospel, however imperfectly I have lived up to it, was and is enough. But the two thoughts which God has given me all my life have been – First to infuse the mystical religion into the forms of others (always thinking they would show it forth much better than I) especially among women, to make them 'handmaids of the Lord'. Secondly to give them an organisation for their activity in which they could be trained to be 'the handmaids of the Lord'.

On death

In 1902, Lady Stephen told Florence Nightingale that a mutual friend had died and was 'at rest'. Florence sat up in bed: 'Oh no,' she said, 'I am sure it is an immense activity.'

2 Writings from Egypt

Evil and good
From 'Letters from Egypt'. During her journey to the Nile over the winter of 1849–50, Florence Nightingale visited the Temple of Athor, built by the great Rameses of the nineteenth dynasty, who reigned 1,350 years before Christ:

> The slanting lines of the face of the temple (none of them parallel) are ugly, and the six colossal figures between the slants impossible to see, as the bank slopes straight down from the temple to the river. Yet I have a love for the place; it is so innocent, so childish, so simple. ... One only of the representations [inside] interested me much. It was the great Rameses crowned by the good and the evil principle on either side. What a deep philosophy! – what theory of the world has ever gone farther than this? The evil is not the opposer of the good, but its *collaborateur* - the left hand of God as the good is His right. I don't think I ever saw any thing which affected me more than this (3,000 years ago) – the king at his entrance to life is initiated into the belief that what we call the evil was the giver of life and power as well as the good. ... In these early temples, the evil spirit is the brother, not the foe of Osiris. Afterwards, he is carefully scratched out whenever he appears; but in the early times of our own Bible, Satan was one of the servants of God, not His enemy (as we have made him), and comes with the *other*

sons of God in Job, to give account of what he has been about and to receive his comrades. Like the Satan of Job seems to me to have been the evil Spirit of the early Egyptians. Necessary to the system of divine providence his influence was considered a benefit. Nothing was put into us in vain; but every thing in us which we consider bad was only an excess either of reason, feeling or conscience, and when properly balanced by the other, would become good ... the old Egyptian believed that out of good came forth evil, and out of evil, came forth good; or as I should translate it, out of the well-ordered comes forth the inharmonious, the passionate; and out of disorder, again order, and both are a benefit.

Afterlife
From 'Letters from Egypt':

I have often thought there is much more evidence for a future world than there is for this. For the existence of this [world], we can only draw evidence from our perception ... for the existence of another, we can draw evidence from our reason, our feeling, our consciousness. ... But the Egyptians seem to have gone farther; they seem to have said, we will consider this life as interesting only in its connection with the whole of which it is a part. I have often thought how dull we were not to see that Christ's life showed this more advanced stage of existence which we call heaven; how we have persisted in calling him 'the man of sorrows', instead of calling him the man who is already in a state of blessedness, the man who has progressed and succeeded.

1850. Extract from 'Visions of Temples', a fictional meditation on the history of Egypt, in the style of Ecclesiastes (then thought to have been written by Solomon) as if written by Rameses the Third. Inspired by Florence Nightingale's visits to ancient temples, it describes how 'after centuries of purification', the spirits of Egyptian kings return to look upon their monuments:

> And the spirit of the first Sethos was sent upon the earth –
> And he built a temple to the one God [Temple of Karnac], the Great Unknown, the Unutterable, the Infinite Himself, to Him to whom a thousand years are but as a day, and a day as a thousand years, to Him who creates Good and Evil, who has formed darkness as well as light.
>
> And he said, Shall we have nought that is evil, have nought but the enervating good? Nay, but even with God, impossibilities are possible. Can man have the good of patience without suffering? have the good of happiness, and the good of suffering, and both from happiness? Can he be taught without evil? the law he is to learn without enduring the consequences that it has caused?
>
> But without consequences, there would be no law.
>
> Let us have evil, he cried, O my God.
>
> And he caused himself to be represented gifted with life by the two Spirits of God, Good and Evil, that all the people might see their King accepted suffering.

3 Extracts from Essays Published in Her Lifetime

Heaven on Earth

May 1873. From 'A Note of "Interrogation"', *Fraser's Magazine*:

> A very great deal of what is untrue to fact and to feeling is talked, for instance, as to belief in a future state that this is 'instinctive', 'intuitive', the fruit of the natural craving of man etc., etc. We do not see such 'craving'. On the contrary. There is perhaps no one subject interesting himself on which the ordinary man thinks so little. Of the best men there are now many would rather *not* have a future state. ...

People, she continues, who have consecrated themselves to the good of others are generally very sensitive. And the strain of that

> produces that condition of mind – so far more common (at least in this age) than any ecstasies of the saints – that longing, not to live for ever, but to die for ever, to be at rest. ...
>
> Mankind must make heaven before we can 'go to heaven' in this world or in any other. ...
>
> It's said of the French soldier in an expeditionary force that he always wants to know where he is going, what he is doing, why he is suffering. Except on this condition of

letting him know this, you will not get out of him all he can give.

And if any can justly be called an expeditionary force, it is surely the expedition of mankind sent by God to conquer earth, to conquer perfection, to create heaven!

And how can man give his best unless he knows ... what is God's plan for him in this world and the next – why there are such sufferings in the world – who is this God who has put him here, and why He has put him here, and put here to suffer so much?

The Problem of Evil
May 1873. From 'A Note of "Interrogation"', *Fraser's Magazine*. Infection, Florence Nightingale argues, is a way of stirring man up to social improvement:

> The lesson of 'infection' is to remove the conditions of dirt, of over-crowding, of foulness of every kind under which men live ...
>
> Disease is Elijah's earthquake, which forces us to attend, to listen to the 'still small voice'. May we not therefore say that 'infection' (facts and doctrine) shows God to be a God of love?

Social religion
July 1873. From 'A sub-"Note of Interrogation"', *Fraser's Magazine*:

> To Christ, God was everything – to us he seems nothing, almost if not quite nothing, or if he is anything, He is only the God of Sundays, and only the God of Sundays as far as

going to what we call our prayers, not the God of our week-days, our business, and our play, our politics, and our science, our home life and our social life; our House of Commons; our Government; our post office and correspondence, our Foreign Office and our India Office.

4 Florence Nightingale's Creed

I believe in God the Father Almighty, maker of Heaven and Earth. And in Jesus Christ, his best Son, our Master, who was born to show us the way through suffering to be also His sons and His daughters, His handmen and His handmaidens, who lived in the same spirit with the Father, that we may also live in that Holy Spirit whose meat was to do His Father's will and to finish His work, who suffered and died saying, 'That the world may love the Father.' And I believe in the Father Almighty's love and friendship, in the service of man being the service of God, the growing into a likeness with Him by love, the being one with Him in will at last, which is Heaven. I believe in the plan of Almighty Perfection to make us all perfect. And thus I believe in the Life Everlasting.

5 Nursing as a Spiritual Vocation

Nursing is an Art; and if it is to be made an art, requires an exclusive devotion, as hard a preparation, as any painter's or sculptor's work; for what is the having to do with dead canvas or cold marble compared with having to do with the living body – the temple of God's spirit. It is one of the Arts; I had almost said, the finest of the Fine Arts.

6 Extracts from *Suggestions for Thought to the Searchers after Truth ...*

DEDICATION:
TO THE ARTIZANS OF ENGLAND

Fellow-Searchers,

I come to you not to declare the truth; I come to ask you (if subjects of moral truth have an interest with you) to join in seeking it with those capabilities which God has given to us. I offer the result of my own endeavors, and what I am able to gather from the endeavors of others.

The object of our desire is to be Truth. All should have their faculties exercised and educated, for the purpose of forming a judgment of what is God's truth.

It is thought desirable for all to learn what is necessary to gain a livelihood. Arithmetic and other matters of instruction are taught for this purpose. But education is not pursued altogether with a right spirit and purpose. Man's education should be given for the purpose of regeneration; of putting him in possession of the capability of exercising his powers, so that those powers may reveal to him what, among the labors of mankind after truth, is really truth; may enable him to judge of the nature of God, the nature and destination of man, and how practically to pursue that destination.

But how forlorn, many say, thus to be left without an authority on the awful subject of religion!

We are not left without 'authority.' The Spirit of Truth will be our authority, if we will faithfully seek Him. Can there really have been an 'authority', when such different Gods have been believed in; such different modes of serving God pursued? Truth is, indeed, One; but the only way to 'unity of faith', is a true cultivation of the nature, and a true life in which to exercise it. If this can be discovered, unity of faith will exist.

Moses and Paul came forth from their desert, saying, 'this and this is miraculously revealed truth, which the world is to believe.' Should it not rather be said, 'this is truth, viz., that man is to discover from the means within and without his nature, all the truth to find which that nature is competent?'

We offer you what we believe to be truth. We offer our reasons to your reason, our feelings to your feeling. Judge ye if it is truth.

Do we speak of what is important? Then consider it. Is it important? If not, hear us no further in this matter.

Religion in Victorian England

In this age, atheism and indifference are man and wife. In former times, atheism used to be the father of despair. But now people live without God in the world, and don't so much as know that He is not there: they are not aware of his absence. Formerly, the terror and the anguish of the sceptic testified to what he had lost, and were the truest witnesses to God and to his own *religiousness*. Now, the indifferentist is called the religious man, and the religious man is the heretic.

Indifferentism, satisfied with conventional life, busy in gratifying man's external pleasures, prevails largely. Among the earnest spirits, the resource is, either a return to Roman Catholicism, or 'let us work at our lives, and leave alone this subject of religion, which only makes men quarrel.'

How do you know a religious man now? By his going to church. And going to church is considered as a duty, that is, as something due – to whom? – to God: something you have done for Him; He is flattered by your going to church. But it is not always done as a compliment to Him; sometimes it is done as a compliment to our fellow creatures. Mrs A. is deaf, and cannot hear the service; but she always goes to church for the sake of 'example'. A great many ladies never miss going where they are known, for this purpose; but if they are where they are not known, they do not go. What a poor compliment it is to God to go, not because you have something you want to say to Him, but 'because Mrs A. goes.' In a country church, if there is a wedding of any consequence, the church is always sure to be full the first Sunday the bride appears, in order to see her. 'To see the bride,' is a very innocent amusement; but is religion come to that pass in this country that people go to a place, where they say they expect to meet God, to 'see the bride'?

In more civilized society, a woman scarcely ever leaves a breakfast table to put on her bonnet for church, without hearing a joke among the men and the inquiry, 'Shall *you* go this morning?' 'No, I don't like the Litany. Shall you?' 'Yes, I shall; I don't like shocking our hostess.' And when you meet at luncheon, 'Have you fulfilled your ecclesiastical duties? Oh! shocking; don't you consider it a duty? I did not know you were so bad.' Or 'I counted forty-six people asleep this morning.'

And when one thinks that there are fifteen thousand sermons to be preached this morning, and more than fifteen thousand breakfast tables where similar jokes are making, and this is called a Church, and this religion! ...

Duty is so difficult now; formerly it was quite certain what there was to be done. People were to go to church and teach their children the catechism and the creed, and give away flannel petticoats and broth, which was called 'doing good'; there was no doubt about it. But now it is truly said of many a woman, 'she has been trying all her life to do a little good, and has done a great deal of harm.' People know that giving away is not doing good, and they don't yet know what to do in its place; even such a school as King's Somborne is not doing unmixed good. No more do people know what to teach their children; even the atheists among the operatives cannot bear teaching them that there is *no* God, and yet they do not know *what* God to teach them. A religious woman used to attend 'Divine Service' on Sundays and say her prayers, that was her religion. Her goodness was to be careful of the poor, and to do little kind things by everybody, and further, to make society for her children; about all these things there was no doubt; but now? ...

Good people often say that they are afraid of all these new-fangled doctrines destroying spiritual feeling, cutting off communication with God. But what have they now? what communication have men, have gentlemen, with God? They go to church because their wives make them, and criticize the sermon a great deal, and they have prayers with the servants in the morning, because their wives wish it; but no one ever thinks of this religion as a religion for men, but as one for women and children. ...

The feeling of the Church of England is very intelligible. Many know that they are in a state of 'twilight faith'. But what can they do? If they stop out of it, they step into a state of darkness. They have not admitted the principle, 'Search', and it is like stepping out of a rickety house into the blank cold darkness of unbelief.

Is it not possible that this sense of uncertainty it is which has led so many lately into the Roman Catholic Church, and some the most learned, the most earnest? Scepticism, not belief, has brought them there. They required their sense of a truth to be stronger and more complete than it was. The more they urged themselves to believe, the less real was their feeling of belief, till, at last, they took refuge in the belief of others to supply that which they had not in themselves.

In this age, however, by far the greater proportion of mankind, have gone the other way; in England, most of the educated among the operatives, especially in the northern manufacturing towns, have turned their faces to atheism or at least to theism – not three in a hundred go to *any* place of worship; the moral and intellectual among them being, almost without an exception, 'infidels'. What the most conscientious among our working men seem to be doing now, is renouncing religious error, not announcing religious truth; they seem not to be seeking after light, but giving up darkness.

These poor fellows, thinking so hard and so conscientiously, leave out the best element in the food which they so earnestly seek; the most divine element, that which makes confusion into order, that which makes the lowest into the highest; for the highest discoverable principle in existence, perhaps, is the feeling residing in the perfect One, which wills happiness; the thought of the perfect One, that happiness is, by its essence, worked out for the happy by exercise of their own natures and of other natures like theirs. *Time* is all that intervenes between man as he is, and man made one with God. ...

The religion of mankind is *without*, outside of them, making them discontented with themselves and their lives, whenever they think of it, but not helping them to improve their lives by themselves, themselves by their lives.

None of the great reformers have ever taken the way of life into account. Wesley – how much in earnest he was! – he preached and people were glad to hear. But did he say to the people, 'Now while you are washing can you be in accordance with God?'

There must be washing, and ironing, and building, the earth must be cultivated; we must have food, and drink, and shelter. How can these occupations be organized so as to be in accordance with God's purpose instead of separating us from it?

Now we have not an idea of being in accordance with God's purpose. We put a great deal of food upon the table, but there is no thought of its being wholesome; there is no calculation of what will give us most strength and vigor to do God's work.

On the contrary, if we send for a physician we know that he will put us on a 'regimen', and give us something quite different. The same as to dress; there is no thought of God's purpose. The same as to occupation.

Fashion directs us; *i.e.*, that which is conventional in our order.

Conventional life consists in this, in saying, 'I am so sorry', 'I hope you are coming', when we are not 'sorry', and we do not 'hope'; in *saying the proper thing without feeling it*. This is the first step in conventional life. The next step is when we actually do not know whether we feel it or not. And the last is when we have said what is 'proper' till we do not know that we do not feel it – when we really think we feel a thing, because we have said it.

A true scheme for mankind would differ from all others in regard to this, that we should organize a life by which it would be possible to live in harmony with God's purpose. But now if we have been with Him in our 'closet', we cease to be with Him as soon as we are at our work or with man, instead of being more with him when at our work, because it is *His* work, and it is more in accordance with His purpose to work than to meditate. But there *is* now no purpose of this kind, and there never has been any purpose of this kind in any of the organizations or religions of nations. We have it set down in our minds that nations are to rise and fall; we make a little vague talk about 'civilization' and 'luxury'; but it is not set down in our minds that a nation living in disregard of God's purpose, when it comes to civilization and the enjoyments of civilization, must fall into selfish indulgence, thence into luxury, thence into decline and ruin.

'Whether ye eat or drink,' says St Paul, 'do all to the glory of God.' Does 'good society' in England eat and drink 'to the glory of God'? 'Good society' in England acknowledges the Bible as inspired; a man is impeded in 'society' if he is known to think otherwise. Yet, if one were to go to the highways of society, on its way to unwholesome and extravagant dinners, and speak forth these words, *that* one would be called a fanatic, and by the very men who would most strenuously oppose the admission into high offices of any one who said that the Bible was *not* peculiarly inspired, and that we are *not* bound to fashion our belief by it.

Such is our belief in this Book which we profess to believe. This is the most singular of all such states of mind, when people abandon that which they do care for, for that which they do not care for. Few care for the Church of England; yet men are sometimes seen giving up a friend whom they like because he does not belong to a Church to which they are indifferent.

Opinions on religion do not *now* model life. The habits of life are stamped in strong and durable fashion. That certain individuals, here and there, differ from orthodox views makes little impression on modes of life. Except in religious orders, the Roman Catholic, the Puseyite, the Evangelical, the Jew, in the higher and middle ranks of life, live much after the same fashion, though in different *coteries* and refraining more or less from each other's society; but their habits do not differ materially or generally according to their religious views. If we study the varying manners of society (in our own country at least), we find them little influenced by religion. That which is called civilization in manners and habits, has it sprung from religion? Convenience and luxury advance from year to year; but does religion prompt them? The manners of the time of Sir Charles Grandison are very different from the manners of to-day. It would be amusing and interesting to spend a day among our ancestors of that date; but has religion influenced those changes? The Quakers speak and dress in certain formalisms, according to the directions of their religious ancestors. The Roman Catholics fast and attend to certain observances. But, generally speaking, is the way in which mankind employ themselves influenced by religion? Is their food, their dress, their conversation influenced by religion? Daily or weekly, on bended knees, at certain prescribed hours, to confess sins, little really felt or thought of – daily or weekly to offer praises and thanks to a Being little understood and little thought of – is not this the chief sign that religion exists at all in English society? In the time of Cromwell and among his followers, could we go back to spend a day with *them*, we should perhaps find a life really influenced by their views of religion; but where could we now track religion in life, *generally* speaking? Individuals will probably present themselves in each generation whose lives have sprung out of their religion; but not generations. ...

What *is* the religion people have now?

'What *is* the religion that people have now?' If they do wrong, they say, Let us pray – pray for pardon and peace. If they have 'trials', as they call them, they say, Let us bear them patiently: in another world it will all come right. If they are well-meaning and conscientious, and they make mistakes, or fail, or are hindered by external circumstances, they say, God takes the will for the deed: in heaven we shall see our hopes fulfilled; – not, There will be no heaven for me, nor for any one else, unless we make it – with wisdom carrying out our thoughts into realities.

   Good thoughts don't make a heaven, any more than

they make a garden. But we say, God is to do it for us: not we. We? – what are we to do? – we are to pray, and to mean well, to take care that our hearts be right. 'God will reward a sincere wish to do right.' God will do no such thing: it is not His plan. He does not treat men like children: mankind is to create mankind. We are to learn, first, what is heaven, and secondly, how to make it. We are to ascertain what *is* right, and then how to perform it ...

It is said that we could have no comfort in our religion if we did not think our prayers were heard and answered.

Surely *that* is the most *uncomfortable* part of it. You say your prayers and you don't know whether God has heard you or not, whether He will answer you or not, nor *why* He has heard you, nor how to bring Him to answer you. Some few feel, from the sensation of comfort and satisfaction in themselves, that He has answered them; other few are miserable because no such feeling in themselves gives them a conviction that He has heard them. The greater part go their way, having 'done their duty' in 'saying their prayers', and never look for any result at all.

This morning I read to my dear grandmother the Psalms for the day, as usual; I sang 'unto the Lord a new song', I sang 'praises unto his name'; 'For why?' as the Psalmist very properly asks; why, indeed? Because the Lord had killed all the young Egyptians, both human beings and animals; because he had favoured the Israelites and proscribed every one else. So do we think now, viz., that He 'hath set apart' the English for Himself, and favoured them to the detriment of every other nation. And, really, that such things should be 'sung and said' by educated men in every church in England 'throughout the year'! Two hundred years hence what will be thought of us? that we ought to have been in a lunatic asylum; but people in lunatic asylums are more sensible. Is it as extraordinary that a man should think himself a teapot as that we should think God like this? ...

People have no God now. A few speculate as an amusement to the intellect, but most have a diluted religion of the kind of St Teresa's. [1] They use the prayers she did, but without expecting the answer she did. They pray for rain, but they look at the barometer and ask which way the wind is. What can you expect of a religion which uses the forms without awaiting the result? They pray indeed, but they don't know whether they shall have it or not. If they have, they are surprised; if they have it not, they say it was not wise to give it them. But our God always does what is wise, whether we suggest it to Him or no. St Teresa was so much better than her God.

The Protestants, it is said, do not feel so much for their purer God as the Catholics do for their unjust one.

But we can hardly call the Protestant God a God at all. What does He stimulate us to do? What does He require of us but to go to church once a week? We cannot say, 'Why are the Protestants not better than the Catholics, their God being so much less absurd?' We can only say, the Protestants have hardly any God at all. They were so occupied with the absurdities of the Roman Catholic God that, as often happens, they did not perceive that they had left themselves no God at all. For the last 300 years, the work of religion has been a work of destruction.

And when will it come to be a work of edification?

Even now we hear 'the voice of one crying in the crowd, "Prepare ye the way of the Lord."' [2] We do not wonder at the rejection of Monotheism on account of its dullness. The Jewish religion and the Unitarian are the dullest of all. They are pure Monotheism. The Catholics, with their angels, and devils, and Saints, and Virgin, and the Holy Ghost, and the Son, do make religion more exciting. But God in his solitary existence, enjoying while we are suffering, is the most cheerless religion – would be revolting, if we really believed what we think we believe. No wonder we turn from him with indifference and then complain of our hard hearts. ...

The Incarnation – the Trinity – the Atonement seem to be abortions of a comprehension of God's plan. The Incarnation? We do not see that God is incarnate in *every* man. We think He was only incarnate in one. We make the Trinity God, Christ and the Holy Ghost – instead of making it God and man, and such manifestation of God as man is able to comprehend.

The Atonement? Man had a dim perception of God passing through sin and suffering for man and in man, and also of sacrifice and compensation – though it seems a curious sort of compensation that His Son should suffer and die because we have offended Him – the whole scheme of grace and redemption appears to be an elaboration of error founded upon some truth. And yet this is believed, and the simple scheme of God's providence men are so scandalized at; it is indeed necessary to have a church to keep up all this.

'How glad we should be, if God *did* speak to us, as St Teresa thought He did,' is often said.

But there is hardly anything which it has ever been *supposed* that God did say, than which we could not have said something better ourselves. What St Teresa says – what Moses says – the ten commandments – are they not full of mistakes? 'I am He that brought thee out of the land of Egypt.' He was taking care of the Egyptians as much as of the Hebrews. 'I the Lord am a jealous God.' The iniquity of the fathers is indeed visited upon the children, but not because God is 'jealous'. The fifth Commandment [3] contains three mistakes, first, we *can* only honour that which is honourable; secondly, filial piety has nothing to do with living to old age; thirdly, the Lord did not give them that land (in the sense in which Moses said it) – they took it. As to 'Thou shalt not kill,' 'Thou shalt not steal,' we did not require a voice from God to tell us that it was better not to kill and steal. Christ does *not* say that God spoke. It shows his great wisdom. But, in the few times when God is said to have spoken in the New Testament, it does not appear that He said anything very inspiring. He said, 'This is my beloved Son, in whom I am well pleased, hear ye Him.' When he speaks to Paul, and says, 'I am Jesus whom thou persecutest,' we feel sure that that is *not* what He would have said. It is true, there is much in the Christian religion which has nothing to do with Christ.

The atonement, the incarnation, these He never preached – nor the ecclesiastical pomp, nor the fabric of the hierarchy.

Nothing, in the vagueness of people, strikes one so much as their raving against the Catholic superstitions, and not seeing that, if the words of Christ were exactly followed out, the Catholic Orders will result – the parting with all they have – the leaving father and mother – all excepting their mortifications, – those He never preached.

The orthodox took hold of a great truth, when they got hold of the incarnation – but they confined it to one – they did not extend it to all. They dwell so much on the passion of Christ, which He suffered for us for a few hours, and they think nothing of the passion of God for eternity – which He suffers for our sakes since the world began. Books upon books have been written upon the day's suffering, till the most fanciful schemes have been built upon it, as might be expected, in order to supply materials for thought. If they would think upon the plan of God, the sufferings of God from eternity, what truths might not be discovered! what mines are there not to be worked! The gospel of a perfect God. What a gospel might be preached!

The 'evangelicals' so often complain of their hard hearts (Wesley's [4] whole tone is of nothing else), they say they cannot love God. Is it any wonder? How can they love the being whom they imagine? They work themselves up by excitement into a kind of spasm of interest about Him; but they must find their hearts hard, in a religion so essentially cold.

It seems to be inconsistent with love and wisdom to have the work and the suffering to any but itself; therefore God works for us in us. The true feeling of *God in us*, which led to the belief of one incarnation, ought to be extended to the incarnation in *all of us*.

The Roman Catholic idea is not nearly so fine as God's thought. But it is the *next* fine idea to it. If God had not done what He has done, He would have done what the Roman Catholics say He has, that is, if He had not made truth discoverable by the exercise of man's faculties, He would have *told* it to man in one continuous line of communication and revelation, as the Roman Catholic church says He has to her. It is curious, however, that the whole cumbrous fabric of contradictions – contradictions to love and wisdom – should be thought right and orthodox, when compared with the simplicity of God's scheme, at which people are 'shocked'.

Mankind have thought a great deal about doing the will of God, but have not thought *what* God is and *what* His will will be – what he will like – when they try to do it.

And now people think less of what will be the will of God than of what will gain the sympathy of men. Now, too, in times when what God likes, and what men will sympathize with are so very different – when, in truth, what God and man will sympathize with, is hardly ever the same thing – this is dangerous indeed.

What is God like?
Ideas make progress. And the meanings attached to words which express ideas cannot, therefore, remain the same.

A house may mean a house in all ages, though even in the case of words which express things, the house which we build now signifies a very different thing from the house built from the painted Briton. How much greater must be the difference in the sense of a word used to express a religious or a political idea! Either we must have new words or new meanings.

The word 'God' has been used to express such various conceptions that there is a degree of vagueness in the proposition, which, however, we admit to be undeniable, since all those conceptions include the idea of super-human power.

It would be the greatest gain religion has ever made, if, for a time, the word *God*, which suggests such various and irreverent associations (irreverent, that is, to a spirit seeking right) could be dropped – and the conception substituted of a perfect being, the Spirit of Right.

Here we come to consider the meaning or rather the meanings with which the word 'God' is used. It has been used to signify the most different ideas in different ages and nations. Can you attach any similarity of idea to the God whom his people whipped to make him do what they liked and to the God who sat enthroned in the mystic phrase of Zoroaster? Nothing is more common than to say, there never has been a race nor an age which did not believe in a God. A god certainly. But *what* God? What does the word mean? A cat? – a lamb? – a spirit? – a statue? These words are as synonymous as the different Gods in which different races and different ages of the same race have believed. When you ask, Why do you believe in God? I must ask, Which of the ideas of God do you mean? whether the God of the Old Testament, who commanded the extirpation of the Canaanites? or the God of the New Testament, who commanded submission to the yoke in many things in which, as we worship Him now, we believe that He commands the struggle for freedom?

The God 'of Abraham, of Isaac, and of Jacob' was certainly *not* the God 'of the whole earth'. It is true that the Hebrews *served* but Him alone; they *believed*, however, in the existence of many Gods. Their own God they reverenced, and despised the other Gods. But it was not till long afterwards that they rose with increasing knowledge to the belief that there was but one supreme. ...

It is evident that every nation, every age, *could* not believe in a Perfect Being – that it required cultivation, development to conceive the idea of perfection, and that the higher all the faculties of an individual, as also of a nation, have been, the higher has been his conception of God, the nearer perfection. ...

But we must be careful to know that the God whom we believe in *is* a perfect being. Men often think that they believe in a perfect God when, in fact, they do not – when they are really wholly incapable of even conceiving of a perfect being. For instance, in the earlier nations, where revenge was considered a virtue in man, it would naturally be thought so in God. Many imperfections, as we now think them, were once deemed virtues, and consequently attributed to a God who was *called* perfect.

Authority does not teach belief in a perfect God. It is evident that very few have believed that their God was perfect. Some nations have not professed to do so; others have attributed to him qualities essentially imperfect, while giving him the title of perfect. For instance, the Greeks did not suppose their Zeus, Athene, etc. perfect. They attributed to them merely human qualities with superhuman power. Athene was the goddess of wisdom, not the wise goddess. Themis was the goddess of justice, not the just goddess. So our Perfect Being is goodness, is wisdom, is power.

In these earlier nations, *power* seems to have been the principal characteristic of a God. He or she was merely an engine to account for creation. Take all the thousand different meanings, which have been attached to the word 'God' by different nations and individuals in different ages, and some kind and degree of power above human seems to be all that is common to them. In these days we profess that we believe our God to be perfect, but we attribute to him all kinds of qualities that are not – love of His own glory, anger, indecision, change of mind – and we try to believe, if we think at all, that a God with these qualities is perfect.

Man's conscious weakness, the terrible sufferings he has endured which he has been powerless to prevent, the intensity of his desire for what he cannot obtain, his imperfect conception of moral right, have confused might and right. Power to do what he cannot do has been his God.

The earliest and still recurring question of man concerning the Superhuman Power which he dimly recognizes seems mainly to have been how to obtain that this Power shall assist his desires, relieve his sufferings. He does not conceive of this Power as acting on a principle, or according to a rule. He attempts to propitiate Him by offerings, by sacrifice, by glorification, by prayer; or, believing in the moral nature of God, he supposes human suffering the result of God's displeasure for man's sinfulness. He believes, for instance, that cholera may be removed by man's repentance for sin, averted by his refraining from it. He has not recognized that to the virtuous or the vicious cholera is incident in certain states of body, under certain circumstances. ...

The question, Why we believe that there exists at all an Eternal Spirit of perfect goodness, wisdom, and power, I can only answer, By experience, and experience only. What mankind can learn of the past, the present, and the future is in harmony with the existence of such a spirit; without it, is unaccounted for. In earlier ages it was thought that what we see about us could not be accounted for, except by supposing imperfect qualities in the Eternal

Spirit. But if, – as we make progress, we find a great many marks that He is perfect – if by degrees we should find that that very evil, which had made us *doubt* His perfection, is one of the truest proofs of it, shall we not come at last to think that He has done in the universe what we should have done, had we been perfect?

Thus increased knowledge, knowledge of the laws of God, is essential to our forming this idea of His perfection. Although a man in a dark room may often form a truer idea of Him than a philosopher observing the rotation of the sun, still, besides a man's *feeling* of what is *right*, his power of comprehending providence depends on his knowledge of the past, the present, and the future.

If it be said that this is reducing the wise and good God to the measure of my own understanding and heart, I answer, Not to mine, but to the accumulated and accumulating experience of all mankind.

What is the meaning of the word 'religion'?

What is the meaning of the word 'religion'? Is it not the tie, the *binding*, [5] or connexion between the Perfect and the imperfect, the eternal and the temporal, the infinite and the finite, the universal and the individual?

The essence of religion is love of a living good and true and right, – veneration, admiration, trust, sympathy in a good and true and right above human.

The primary fact in religion seems to be the existence of an omnipotent spirit of love and wisdom – the *primary* fact, because it is the explanation of every other.

This gives us four words to explain, each of which is open to great misconception, and has been greatly misconceived; viz., omnipotent, spirit, love, wisdom.

By *omnipotence* we understand a power which effects whatever would not contradict its own nature and will.

By *spirit* we understand a living thought, feeling, and purpose, residing in a conscious being.

By *love* we understand the feeling which seeks for its satisfaction the greatest degree and the best kind of well-being in other than itself.

By *wisdom* we understand the thought by which this satisfaction is obtained.

How is it revealed?

There have been three parties – those who have said that there was revelation through the book; those who have said that there was a revelation through the Church, or through the book and the Church; and those who have said that there was no revelation at all. Now we say that there is a revelation to everyone, through the exercise of his own nature – that God is always revealing Himself.

Let us suppose that we give up the usual means of receiving truth from church or book, and that we seek it from God through our own faculties, including the spiritual, the affectional, the intellectual, and the physical; and including what these can receive from God by means of the same faculties in mankind as well as in our individual selves. It seems important that the thinkers of the present day (men disgusted with church and book as authority) should be fully aware of this understanding, however, that from book and church we may learn, inasmuch as therein is also to be found exercise of human faculty.

We believe that *all* the faculties of all mankind should be exercised to receive the revelation of God to man. The

Roman Catholic, the Anglican, etc., etc., etc., exercise a very limited number of faculties in what they receive as revelation.

If the eye is diseased, we see falsely; if the reason, feeling, etc., are so, we judge and feel untruly. In both cases we must take care to keep our sources of information in a healthy state. 'If thine eye be single thy whole body shall be full of light.' 'If any man shall do His will, he shall know of the doctrine whether it be of God or not.' If you will carry your belief into your practice you will soon find out whether it is true.

We agree with the Roman Catholic, that is dreadful to be without authority. But we *have* authority. Is not God Himself authority? We are but the vessels. He fills them; and we must keep the vessels unsoiled and pure.

It is said that those who do not admit 'authority' do not know *when* it is God that speaks, and when it is the excitement of a cup of coffee – that they cannot tell whether their vessel be pure. Swedenborg's was pure, and St Francis of Assisi's was pure, yet they came to different conclusions. We may naturally be mistaken in what God says to us, because we have to construct for ourselves and each other the vessel into which the Holy Ghost enters, and often inevitably it becomes occupied with other ghosts. It is truly remarkable, indeed, how some have believed that Christ said to them what they said to themselves, and this with the printed book before them. Little, indeed, does that book probably represent Christ – as little as other books of men's sayings and doings represent *them*. Still, it assures us that he did not think what he has since been said to have thought.

Will it be said that it is presumption and conceit for a

85

few individuals to think that they can discover the true nature of religion, and how it ought to be manifested in life? There is no fear of such presumption, for according to the nature of things, no such conceptions would come into the mind of individuals till *mankind* had been long, long and laboriously at work. Comte profoundly teaches that the errors in man's view of religion are essential paths to truth – they have been no wild vagaries, independent of law. Our heads and our hearts should estimate them with the respect and affection due to them. While we sift truth from falsehood in books held sacred, which have come down to us, let us estimate the value of the truth – the truthfulness, *in its position* as to time and place, of the falsehood. How short-sighted, feeble, and vain is he who fancies *himself* individually to have discovered anything! How disgusting is the narrow selfish folly of A, who is contending in angry pages that he, and not B, made a certain discovery! Be assured it was neither A nor B – it was mankind, it was God in man. The perceptions or ideas in A's mind could never have arisen had not a thinking and laborious race preceded him. When, therefore, you strive in the glorious work of endeavouring to read the revelation of the Great Spirit in time and space, fear not to be presumptuous in using the capabilities which that Spirit has bestowed for this very purpose; fear not that you are arrogating to yourself a power above other men. All science, all history and experience of human nature, which the ages of man have laid before you, are your means for discovery.

'The Church of England is a good human help,' it is said. What does she offer as help? She has certain prayers taken from the Roman Catholic, which, if you find that they suit your feeling too, you may go and hear every

Sunday; twice, if you like; in some places every day; and you may hear the Bible read, which some say you can do just as well at home; and you may hear a sermon preached by the best educated in the land, educated in classical literature, Aristophanes and Cicero, and such theological learning as we can give. Few *men* attend to the sermon, but they may criticize it. Farther, you may be married, that is, have a form of words pronounced over you, which makes your marriage the law of the land; and you may be buried, or the feelings of your friends gratified by having certain words read over you; and when you are ill you may send for the clergyman to read a service by you; and you may receive the sacrament once a month; and your children may be baptized. This is the help the Church offers, which we may take if we like it.

The Church of England has for men bishoprics, archbishoprics, and a little work (good men make a great deal for themselves). She has for women – what? Most have no taste for theological discoveries. They would give her their heads, their hearts, their hands. She will not have them. She does not know what to do with them. 'You may go to the Sunday school, if you like it,' she says. But she gives no training even for that. She gives neither work to do for her, nor education to do it, if she had it to give. Many women would willingly give her their life's work. Luther gave us 'faith,' justification by faith, as he calls it; and the Church of Rome gives us 'works'. But the Church of England gives us neither faith nor works. She tells us neither what to believe nor what to do.

But the Church of England may make discoveries, may make progress, it is said. The Roman Catholic Church cannot.

The Church of England is no training for a discoverer in religious truth; we might as well say that a mathematician is prepared to enter upon farming, as that a man trained in Latin and Greek, and theological learning, is prepared to find out truth in religion. When we walk through the new House of Commons, those rooms do not look like the rooms of an assemblage of men straining to find out truth for a great country, political truth, or the good of a nation. Nor does the Church look like an assemblage of men fitted to find out religious truth.

If it is asked, 'Are we capable of finding out truth?' it may be answered, that what we *might* be is indicated by moments. We are surprised to find the depths of feeling we are capable of. If life were organized so as to produce constantly what we are now conscious of at moments, 'eye hath not seen' that which man might do. And, instead of talking about man being 'desperately wicked', we should say, as we sometimes do say of great heroes, we did not know of what man was capable. Instead of that hideous hopeless repetition every day for years of 'there is no health in us', we should be living with a purpose, a purpose of moral improvement, which would be constantly realized till we were 'perfect, even as God is perfect'. What a difference there is between those thus living with a purpose and those who live with no purpose at all! These take up a book, but not with any particular object to further. They have no purpose but amusement.

The Bible – a final appeal?

Were we in geography or astronomy to take one book as our final rule, our ultimate appeal, the same thing would happen inevitably as has happened in religion. Some things in it we should absolutely ignore, as when we ignore that Solomon said, 'Man is like the beasts that perish'; and of other things we should say, 'he did not mean that – he meant something else'; as when Christ says, 'Hate your father and mother, sell all, and follow me.' No one would cry out so much as the bibliolaters – 'what a shame!' if we were to *do* it; but they say 'he did not *mean* it.' Could we go on with such a system in geography or astronomy?

And yet there are things which nobody does really believe. Suppose I were to say, 'consider the laurel of the garden, how it grows! It toils not, neither does it spin. Do you do like the laurel, and you will have food and clothing too.' People answer, Christ did not mean that, he meant something else. Yet such is the vagueness of men, that this is preached one day in the seven, and the other six days the board of guardians preaches something quite different.

The people look and see, and they see that practically the guardians are right, and that Christ was wrong, and some are frightened and say, 'I have lost my Christ'; and others are hardened and say, 'I don't want your Christ'. These are two alternatives, equally unsatisfactory; but if we put in juxtaposition with this 'the kingdom of Heaven is within', or some other of the truly divine things which Christ has said, and feel that after all there was no one like him, none who knew so much truth as he did, none who lived as he lived – then we are neither hardened nor frightened; we do not lose the truth, and we have not to lie to ourselves about the untruth; we can truly say, never man spake as he spake.

Many who do not believe Christ miraculously inspired

do not become hardened about him; they love him more that ever they did; they admire his life and character more than those do who think him God.

But many men who never read the Bible, because their common sense resists such things as 'Take nothing for your journey, neither scrip, nor staff, neither bread, nor money, nor even two coats'; [6] and 'Shake off the dust against any who do not receive you'; things which belong to the times of the Essene communities, but not to these, and which do not even sound perfectly just and good, as belonging to *those* times – men who cannot bear to read these things, will yet be shocked at not thinking Christ divine. Divine? We too think him divine as all men are divine, but not the *only* divine One. As he said himself, 'those are Gods or the sons of God to whom the word of God comes.'

Universal law – what is it?
The whole state of the universe at this moment is the consequence of the whole state of the universe at every past moment, both as regards its spiritual and its physical laws. God does not will 'on Monday it shall rain, on Tuesday the wind shall be East', or 'the spring of 1852 shall have three months' drought', by an arbitrary decree. The drought of 1852 is the consequence of His meteorological and other laws which have ruled since eternity; not, as in those noble words, 'As it was in the beginning, is now, and ever shall be, world without end,' but As it was *without* beginning, is now, and ever shall be.

Now, when we read Dalton's [7] discovery that all is by weight and measure, that the proportions in which bodies combine follow a numerical law, as, for instance, carbon expressed by 6 unites with oxygen expressed by 8, and forms carbonic oxide – it will otherwise unite only with oxygen expressed by 16, and form carbonic acid, etc., etc. – when we discover such and similar laws, does it not seem that there must be a spirit of wisdom? God is so accurate, so definite; He knows exactly how long we shall go on in a given way, just as He knows how much of the oxygen will combine with carbon, hydrogen, etc.

I once saw an extraordinary storm on the Nile. The river seemed flowing bottom upwards; the whirlwind of sand from the desert literally covering it, and blowing up in ridges upon it. The Israelites might have almost passed upon dry land. Our eyes, mouths, and ears were filled with sand, and it was impossible to drink, for, instead of water from the river, we drew up sand. To try to stand against the wind was useless. Presently five vessels floated past us, keel uppermost, and we saw a little whirlpool of oranges, the unfortunate passengers having broken open the cabin in their efforts to escape. At 3 p.m. it became quite dark, and the waves were like a moderate sea in the Channel. The Arabs thought that the day of judgement was at hand, and were quite helpless.

Now, we know that there was not one molecule of sand or water in that confused whirlwind, which was there by chance, which had not a sufficient cause, so to speak, for occupying the place which it did, which was not rigor-ously where it ought to be, according to the laws or uniform rules of God.

> No atom of this turbulence fulfills
> A vague and unnecessitated task,
> Or acts but as it must or ought to act.

In other words, a natural philosopher, who knew the acting forces and the properties of the atoms acted upon, would demonstrate that each atom acted with precision in the way it ought to act, and could not act otherwise than as it did.

In the terrible convulsions which have shaken Europe, have upset empires and annihilated liberty, there has not been one single action, one single word, one single thought, or will, or passion, in the destroyers or the victims, which was not the infallible sequence of its antecedent, which had not uniformly its allotted succession or coexistence in this moral whirlwind. An intellect which could appreciate the acting forces and the character of the nations acted upon could have demonstrated like a Q.E.D. the results.

Miracles – true or false?

Generally, as the belief in miracles decreases, God dies out. At first, as is very natural, while the laws of God are little, or not at all, understood, people are expecting and finding miracles every day, and see God in them. The Saints lived in a perpetual expectation of a miracle; they speak to God, He hears and answers; and the state of such persons is truer than the state of the assertors of law is now. Trust in the God who will work a miracle in answer to their prayers, veneration for the God who works the miracle, thankfulness, love to Him for having worked one (though we may feel we could not love a God who did work miracles), are truer feelings, juster appreciations of Him, than the appreciation given by the 'positive' school of the present day. Alas! that, as the belief in miracles dies out, *God dies out also.*

All religions have been hitherto founded on miracle – on the breaking of law. The present is an attempt to preach religion founded on 'law' – to make God's law His Gospel – His 'good news' to man.

Had it not been for the miracles and resurrection of Christ, would the Christian religion have been founded? Would the Mahometan religion have been founded without the miracles of Mahomet? [8] Would the pure, devoted and beautiful life of Christ, His doctrines and teaching have laid the corner stone for Christian religion without His resurrection?

No, this is the first attempt to found a religion upon 'law'. The Christian doctrines [i.e., without the belief in miracles] would never have founded the Christian religion.

Much attention has been excited, both in devotion and derision, by the Rimini miracle. The beauty of the picture which people call the 'winking madonna,' and which was 40 years in that small church unobserved, is striking; the expression of purity, holiness, devotion, and melancholy in those up-turned eyes exceeds that of any Madonna, excepting, perhaps, the Dresden Raphael.

But the decaying faith of the town has revived; the besetting sin, swearing, has disappeared, and many conversions have taken place. 'It may be the effect of color' has been said, but is it not equally God's way of calling and awakening souls that He, after a lapse of 40 years, should cause the effect to be seen with such results? must we not look with deep reverence on the instrument through which he has worked such a change?

The most striking part of this story is the state of the people which it shows. The picture had been there 40 years, and had remained unnoticed, the 'purity, holiness, and devotion' said nothing to them; the beauty of virtue had no effect. *This* did not appear to them to be God speaking to them; but is most affecting how ready they were to listen directly, as soon as they thought that they received God's communication in His 'winking' at them. They did not see God in the expression of 'purity and holiness', but they saw Him when the picture shut its eyes. God, acting by a law of goodness and righteousness which *never* fails, is really more worthy of reverence than God 'winking' at us occasionally, or turning water into wine or into blood, or anything else. It is a most curious fact that a picture making faces should have cured swearing, and a most touching one, that the swearers should have been so willing to listen as soon as they could hear. But that which it tells most loudly is, that this people must be raised and educated till they can hear God's voice in His law of perfect righteousness, hear it in everything – that 'still small voice', rather than hear it only in a '*tour de force*'.

People think that they hear God's voice in a miracle now and then; they don't think they hear it in the daily and everlasting expression of His goodness, in the beauty of holiness, in His laws, which are never broken; this *is* very remarkable.

But it is alarming to think how completely we are destitute of the first principles of knowledge with regard to God's nature and His plans with men, His manner of acting. As, till Bacon's time, people were ignorant of the first principle of philosophy, we want a Bacon for the science of God. The crane on Cologne cathedral stands there a monument of man's ignorance of the ways of

God. It was taken down, and there was a thunderstorm. They thought God was offended and put it up again.

But, it is said, it is only the most ignorant who have so absurd a superstition as this.

Is it a whit more absurd than the expecting an 'answer to prayer', which is expecting that God will alter his laws, His *good* laws, in conformity with our advice – and this when all is as certain as an eclipse? If we prayed that the eclipse set down in our almanacs should not take place, would this be more absurd than praying that one of God's *moral* laws should be altered? Is the crane at Cologne a whit more absurd than the theory of forgiveness and absolution?

People are terrified at the idea of a religion without miracles, and belief in miracles certainly makes some happy. It has a cheerful effect to be expecting an inter-position every day; but what a lowering of the conception of God!

In all physical things God's law is invariable. We know that if we eat nightshade we shall perish. We take means that our children shall not eat nightshade; we dig it out of our gardens. We don't pray that it may *not* take effect.

We know that certain organizations in certain circum-stances will become criminal. The law is invariable. Why do we not take means as in the former case? Why do we, instead of this, think that God will alter his righteous law, his invariable law – by the invariableness only of which we can learn – for our prayer?

Without the belief in miracles, in prayer, in a man-God, it is said, we can never have that fervent conviction which St Teresa had.

We open a book of science, and we read of a God all

order and beauty and goodness, and He excites no feeling. We open the life of St Teresa, and we find a God all injustice and disorder, and we find her in a rapture about Him. The God of law is always speaking to us – always saying what is wise and good. The God of St Teresa speaks to her sometimes, and says something which is often foolish and not good. Curious indeed, that, while the God of science never appears to have excited any feeling, the other God has excited so much! May we not hope that the day is coming when we shall feel as much, yea, a great deal more for our God than she did for hers?

Our creed may be felt a dull one by those who have been used to be kept alive by the belief of past miracles, and, in some sort, to look for present ones – since they expect their prayers for restoration of health, for rain or fair, to be answered.

Mankind, however, are not *now* much kept alive by belief in miracles. St Teresa believed, with her whole soul, the miracles which she relates. But do the many congregations which listen on the appointed day to what was said by Balaam's ass really believe that it spoke? Or, when the same congregation pray for fine weather or for rain, is there a real expectation that any effect from these prayers will result? Is there much vitality in the forms of prayer by law appointed? The religion of the Church of England is mainly now the religion of order, decency, respect. It is probably much better than none; but of how much more is not humanity capable!

Religion now tells of an occasional miracle, meaning an occasional effect produced by the immediate will of God. We believe *all* successions, all co-existences to be, in this sense, miraculous. We believe there is no reason, no cause for *any* succession, *any* co-existence other than the will of God.

The beliefs of man have come from the assertions of individuals of their own feelings. The multitude has been led by those who felt fervently. These feelings have been stereotyped, and have been held, after all feeling had departed from the words and practices which once betokened feeling.

Remember these words, 'Lo, it is I, be not afraid.' Some great artist should paint a series of pictures, where man is passing through sorrow, and God says, 'It is I, be not afraid'; where he is passing through sin, even through sin – yes, *most* through sin, and God says, 'It is I, be not afraid.' God is so much more there than 'walking on the sea', which is, after all, very paltry. Raphael paints Him performing the miracle of the fish, and makes him so divine that we lose sight of the absurd nature of the miracle. But, if he had painted him saying to man in a state of sin and degradation, 'It is I, be not afraid', how much more divine!

People make such a point of having the evidence of eye-witnesses to a miracle. But here we have the evidence of St Teresa that she saw two little devils round a priest's neck. We have the evidence of St Paul that he saw a light in the sky, and heard a voice. We are as certain of their honesty, we are as certain that they believed it, when they said they saw the devils and the light, as I am that I believe it when I say I see an ink-stand on the table. There is no more ground for suspecting imposture in the case of St Paul than in that of St Teresa; but that the devils were not there, and that the voice was not there, we are equally certain. Therefore, what is the 'evidence' of an 'eye-witness'?

Wherever miracles have been believed, they have been seen. We feel as sure that St Teresa believed she saw the miracle as that she did not see it. There is no difference in our certainty.

The time is coming when, more and more, others as well as ourselves, will discern the little dependence to be placed on supernatural revelation; consequently, let us search to the utmost the *real* grounds man will have for a religion when the unreal grounds crumble away beneath him. The divinities of Greece and Rome, how powerful they were! But they are laid low. Hardly a trace of belief in them remains. The belief in all supernatural foundation for religion will give way in like manner. ...

When law was traced in astronomy and geology, Genesis ceased to be authority in those sciences. When law is traced in the history of events, and in moral philosophy, Christ will no longer be considered as supernatural authority, speaking, as He does, of providential interference and forgiveness of sins. And when this day comes, where will be our religion? Religion *might* be more felt, more comprehended, infinitely more influential on life than it ever has been.

It is said that Christ is God. But there is wanted a higher God than Christ, a higher God than even Christ's God. Certainly Christ believed that he could work miracles. Can we believe that such would be a God whom we can feel veneration for, whom we can trust in? The God of law is surely a much higher God than this. The God who works miracles is not the highest. We want the *Most* High.

God's plan is to teach all by invariableness. See how opposed this is to miracles, which teach by variableness!

And how are we ever to learn when we cannot be sure of what is coming?

When Christ says, 'faith shall remove mountains', he appears to think that if you can but believe it, God will break a law. For to remove a mountain in the way He implies would be to break a law. No doubt the expression was used merely as a strong and startling one. But he would not be a wise man who would wish to break a law of God. He would be the wise man who believes that God will *never* break His laws, not that, if *he* believes that God will, He will. Certainly Christ's was not the God of Law.

But some think that the theory of omnipotent and implacable *law* is not more satisfactory than that of benevolent caprice, the recognized form of Deity. They think this a miserable world. If they are to be miserable, it does not signify to them whether they are miserable in consequence of such misery being the law, or whether they are miserable in consequence of such misery being the caprice of the Superior Being. On the contrary, they would rather it were caprice, because then there might be some hope that the caprice might change, whereas, if it were the law, there would be no hope.

But it makes some difference *what* the Being is from whom emanates the law. If the law emanates from Juggernaut, certainly we would rather have caprice. But, if the law springs from wisdom and goodness, had we not rather have invariable law?

If it is wisdom and goodness that I and all the world should work out perfection, and that perfection cannot be worked out without ignorance and mistake and misery, does it not *then* make a difference to us whether we are governed by law or caprice?

We must know the purpose of the artist, before we can appreciate his performance. If human physical ease were God's purpose, He has failed. Is it proved that He has failed, if His purpose is a habitation on the heavenly bodies for the exercise of goodness, benevolence, wisdom, righteousness in man? for the attainment of perfection by imperfection, of knowledge by ignorance?

Humans as God's co-workers

Let us understand that *our power* arises from God's invariableness.

We can never too forcibly remember that, because what has been in the past could not have been otherwise, it by no means follows that we are powerless over the present and future.

If we can and *if* we will alter those specific conditions out of which past evil arose, it certainly *will not* recur.

Granted that certain circumstances invariably involve one definite constitution of the human physical being, whence springs the whole capability of that being – granted that circumstances invariably affect definitely this being, so that all he is results from law – is this necessity? is this making him a machine? is it not accordance with right? is it not putting power into his hands? For he has capability to find out how to bring about right physical being – right circumstances in which to live.

While Director-General Andrew Smith [9] was in power, it was 'the gate to the kingdom' of the Army Medical Department to say that yellow fever was an 'inscrutable dispensation', and that nothing could be done to avert it.

Many have believed that cholera was traceable to no other origin than the direct will of superhuman power that it should exist; and the means attempted to prevent it were prayer, which, it was hoped, would influence God's will, or some changing of circumstances totally irrelevant to the case.

This divine will is now shown, by experience and observation, to be that wherever certain physical conditions (such as want of draining, of cleanliness, etc.) exist, cholera, in epidemic years, will exist; that these physical conditions ceasing to exist, cholera will cease to exist.

Buckle says, 'In India slavery – abject, eternal slavery – was the natural state of the great body of the people, the state to which they were doomed by physical laws utterly impossible to resist.'

Granted, so long as circumstances rule man. But God's laws will teach man to rule *circumstances*.

'Thou shalt not kill' is said to be God's law; but this is not God's law, for men *do* kill; while God's law is never broken. Men *do* kill, and if they *could* not kill, there would indeed be no 'liberty'. This is Moses' law, not God's law.

Again, Quetelet shows that not only such a percentage of men *will* kill in a year, but such a percentage out of this percentage will use such a weapon, such a percentage will use poison, etc. This does not show that God decrees that a certain number of murders shall be committed every year, but that certain states of mind, and certain circumstances co-existing, murder will be committed.

Again, it appears that boys between the ages of 15 and 20, although they constitute only one-tenth of the population, afford an amount of crime which constitutes no less than one-fourth of the total crime committed in that population.

But these are the announcements of the statistician, not laws of God.

It is the result of God's law that, given such organizations and such circumstances, given such a state of society, such a number of murderers will there be; and further, such an amount of evil will be entailed on society, teaching it the truth about crime.

It is the result of God's law that, given such a state of society, and such of education, such an amount of boy-crime will take place.

But what is this but to say that we must bring about *another* state of society and of education? ...

With regard to the horrors described in the pages of human history, let us listen to them well. It is the Eternal voice – 'Not so, my Children.' 'Not so' we hear also repeated in every cholera, massacre, vice, degeneration. Man usually replies to it by prayer (if he replies at all), prayer for the removal of the evil. And the Eternal voice answers again, Not so. Cease to spend yourselves in vain. What is this buzz of purposeless talk from thousands of re-unions of such talent as *might redeem* mankind? What is this rattle – ceaseless in your cities yet purposeless for man's divine nature – when such a purpose waits to be fulfilled? Will you stand by, or pursue these inane follies while the divine nature of MAN is being murdered or while he is murdering himself? Or, as inanely, will you betake yourselves to prayers for the salvation of man to Another, whose express plan it is that it shall be your own noble work? The poisoned, the paralysed nature cannot help *itself*. Man must rise up and save.

Human saviours

The world cannot be saved, except through saviours, at present.

Now what are the saviours to do? Not to do anything *instead* of man. Still it is not intended that every man shall learn all the laws of God for himself. In astronomy, Copernicus, Galileo, Kepler, Newton, Laplace, Herschel, and a long line of saviours, we may call them, if we will – discoverers they are more generally called – have saved the race from intellectual error, by finding out several of the laws of God.

In the same way, there may be, there must be saviours from social, from moral error. Most people have not learnt any lesson from life at all – suffer as they may, they learn nothing, they would alter nothing – if they began life over again they would live exactly the same life as before. When they begin the new life in another world, they would do exactly the same thing, and they must, till somebody comes to help them. And not only individuals, but nations learn nothing. A man once said to me, 'Oh! if I were to begin again, how different I would be.' But we very rarely hear this; on the contrary, we very often hear people say, 'I would have every moment of my life over again,' and they think it pretty and grateful to God to say so. For such there can be no heaven; in fact it will not be there for them to have till saviours come to help them. This *is* 'eternal death'.

We sometimes hear of men 'having given a colour to their age'. Now, if the colour is a right colour, those men are saviours.

People think that the world is in the mud, and that it must stay there. We think it is in the mud too, but we are sure it is not to remain there.

The kingdom of God

'Thy kingdom come.' If we seek Christ's most abiding, his uppermost thought, it was this. And what did Christ understand by 'Thy kingdom'? He explains in those memorable words, 'the kingdom of God is within you'. There are no more satisfactory words of His. How much is contained in them! Earth *may* be heaven. But man is of the earth now, and there are so many good and pleasant things now rife in life that man is particularly liable to forget how great he might be – to be satisfied with being an amused and amusing child. Let him arouse himself to a consciousness of the divine within him, as pleasant and cheerful days pass among those around him. It was to the poor the Gospel was preached. And, if another Christ came to draw fresh supplies from the well of truth which fails not, would still speak to the poor. Truth is a *speculation* among the rich. Among the poor, there might be a few who would listen and care to find more truth in life than it now manifests. We must be patient, but never failing in fervour for God's work, ready to work and, which is much harder, ready to wait. Then may some seed be sown in this world, and we may be learning for other spheres, when we cannot learn for this.

What is the origin of evil?

What is the origin of evil? the question so often asked. *The wisdom, goodness, and righteousness of the Perfect, the Father*, is the answer; who wills that Man, the son, by the exercise of his nature in accordance with the laws of right, shall rise from ignorance to truth, from the imperfect to the perfect.

If we inquire into God's dealings with His creatures

with trust that they will be found to arise from goodness and wisdom (since otherwise they would not be God's dealings), we shall come to this question, May not sin have become introduced into the world from ignorance of one or more of God's laws, sin being something untrue in our feelings, our thoughts, our wills; something unlike the feeling, the thought, the will, of God?

How can He cause that which is unlike Himself? may be asked.

As an infant stumbles, and the mother sees it better that it should stumble rather than never learn to walk alone, so it may be said that the stumble is ultimately caused by the mother's will; thus the sin may be caused by the will of God the Father, and yet be unlike His own. Now, all sin arises from ignorance of God's laws at some time or in some individual.

From ignorance? it is asked, when 'I *knew* it was wrong.'

You knew it was wrong to do what you did at a particular time; but there was a time when that in you which led to this sin was called out unknown to you; when there was nothing stronger than it in your character.

With regard to our physical being also, all suffering, all privation of that enjoyment of which man is capable, arises from ignorance of God's laws, either our own ignorance, or that of those who have preceded us.

'Did this man sin, or his parents?'

That question implied a false idea. Sin regards those laws only which concern our spiritual and moral being, that is, our feelings and wills towards God and our fellow creatures. That a man is blind implies some ignorance of physical law, either on his own part or on that of those who preceded him.

Those physical laws may have been disregarded in consequence of something wrong in the spiritual life. Disease in the spiritual being will often lead to indulgence in malpractices in the physical. But the immediate cause of blindness is a physical law. And it is untrue to regard a physical evil as a punishment, that is, an arbitrary infliction for some spiritual evil.

If the question is asked, shall we ever learn all these laws? Do we even know one of them?

In time, that is, in eternity, we shall. God has formed us in the image of himself, and therefore we cannot doubt that man's happiness is to be the same as that of his Father. ...

There will be always evil, because there will be always ignorance. But there will not be always masses of evil, lying untouched, unpenetrated by light and wisdom (in as far as man is concerned), except now and then a temporary improvement by *chance*, not after a type and purpose.

Each advance has always brought evil with good, because each advance must, in some degree, be made upon an hypothesis. But mankind, when they work after a type, will, more and more speedily, turn the evil into good. We shall not wish to part with evil in the abstract, when it is understood to spring from ignorance, when all the faculties of all mankind are directed to expect evil from ignorance, and to remedy it. Then, though it will be the essential attendant on the imperfect and finite in its progress towards perfection and infinity (through exercise of mankind, of *each for each* and *for all*), there will be a perpetual and rapid change of evil into good; thence fresh temporary evil, thence fresh permanent good. And so on, through the universe, through eternity; the Perfect assisting, teaching, giving successive revelations to the imperfect, by His laws which furnish means and inducement by which the imperfect may advance towards the Perfect – thus it has been *without* beginning, is now, and ever shall be.

If we see no evil, the possibility of removing which does not exist in *mankind* (as a whole), why are we to stand wondering that God permits evil? do we want Him to give us no work? or to do our work for us? would that be wisdom, benevolence, love, in Him? Let mankind fulfil its possibilities. That will answer the question; is the existence of evil compatible with the existence of a Being of perfect wisdom and benevolence? When we see a man about to be drowned, saved by the wisdom and kindness of a fellow creature, we do not *then* say, can the Being be benevolent, who allowed man to be liable to be drowned? We admire in Him that He gave the saviour capability for the work of love, that man is saved by the exercise of the capabilities of man, by divine wisdom and love manifested in the 'earthly vessel.'

God has no mysteries for us, any more than the teacher has who commits a problem to his pupil to be worked out, the which could not benefit him but through the exercise of the pupil's own nature. Thus much we know, viz., that a human being, constituted in a certain manner, and that constitution co-existing with certain circumstances, will manifest those attributes, the manifestation of which is all that we know of the Being whom we call God.

We also know that it is in the power of human beings

to affect the constitution and the circumstances of themselves and each other – that, in some instances known to
them, they have power to affect the constitution and the
circumstances of themselves, of their children, of their
fellow creatures, *in such a way* as to increase or lessen the
manifestation of the divine attributes in them.

It is true that the wrong a man does comes from within; that he must undergo suffering or privation till he is
conscious that he is wrong – till that wrong becomes
right. Take the case of disease. That disease arose, partly
from physical circumstances which concerned the beginning of his existence, partly from those after his birth,
before he could have any part in his own destiny; partly
from those after he could know what was right, which
prevented his knowing how to make his volitions right. It
is one thing to know what you ought to do, and another
to know how to do it; one thing to know the law, and
another to know how to incline your heart to keep that
law. But the sick man must be conscious that his physical
frame is in a wrong state, must suffer the consequences
of its being wrong; perhaps during life, perhaps till it
can be put into a right state; and nothing can exempt
him from them.

It is, therefore, a true feeling that the wrong, whether
physical or spiritual, which a man has within himself,
must produce for him suffering, which no one can bear in
his stead.

It is said that it is very hard that man must suffer for
faults which, according to this theory, he could not avoid.

Hard that man should attain to perfect happiness?
Man possesses reason, feeling, conscience, *capable* of
unfolding, so as to be one with God, to think His thought,

to feel as He feels, to will that His will shall be done, and thus to share His happiness, His power. Is this hard? God, it is true, gave him no instinct *how* to cultivate these capabilities aright. Mankind has to learn by experience, 1st, what are his capabilities? 2nd, what are all the various laws of God concerning them? 3rd, that it is desirable to cultivate these capabilities aright; 4th, which of these laws enable him to do so? 5th, how to keep them? 6th, how to incline himself to keep them. All this man has to learn and to practice before he can be one with God.

But the first man had had no experience. He would be *certain* to be ignorant of most of these laws. It would indeed be *impossible* for him to discover them all. It is impossible for us now. Time is the key to God's thought. It is the *word*. In time God's thought is ever being worked out. Without a constant reference to ever passing time, we *must* misunderstand it. It requires united man in all time to discover all. When we pray to be 'kept this day from all sin', to be 'delivered from evil,' we utter a prayer for that which is impossible. [10] Unless we have perfect knowledge of every one of these laws, we *must* err. Our prayer is a contradiction. If we were 'delivered from evil,' the world would be ruined, its only safeguard gone – God's plans are all for eternity.

God has provided that mankind shall attain, therefore, by their own effort to progress towards being as He is and doing as He does.

And if they fail, their will may still be one with His; and this oneness with Him in will shall give comfort where the finiteness of created nature prevents their being and doing as the Infinite.

'Be ye perfect, even as your Father in heaven is perfect.'

Yet will man never be God, but one with God; and when he suffers, he will yet have joy in feeling 'Thy will be done.'

Forgiveness – an unintelligible idea?

What is meant when you say the word 'forgiveness'? People forgive, but how do they do it? Probably they think of something else. If a man knocks me down, and if I feel that he is the greatest sufferer, because he is further from the way of right or happiness by the act of knocking down than I by the act of being knocked down, and if I feel that by the laws of the universe he could not have done otherwise than he did, I can – not forgive, but – feel no resentment, for he could not have done otherwise. But if I am told that I am to forgive another because God forgives me, what have I to do? I must think that that man has been very wrong; but then I have been very wrong, too, against God, and He has forgiven me; and if I don't forgive this man, perhaps another time God will not forgive me. What does that mean? It means that I think of something else, of God's wrath and my sins against Him, and so I forget what has been done against me. Can any other meaning be attached to the theory of forgiveness?

Belief in universal law leaves the word *forgiveness* without a meaning. If it is true that, whatever man has thought or felt, all his inclinations, whatever has been his will, have arisen in accordance with law which it was not in his possibility to annul or to alter, it must be unmeaning to ask God to forgive a past, which arose in accordance with His law, or man to forgive what was inevitable. Anger, indignation against the individual sinner, must be untrue feeling in whatever being it exists.

Forgiveness is certainly a step beyond revenge. In the first state of society, it was considered right to revenge our injuries; in the next state, it was considered right to forgive them; though how this is done we do not know. Still, this is a step in advance. This is already a 'future state' to the first. In the next 'future state' it will be considered that there is nothing to forgive; and that will be a doctrine as much higher and truer than this of forgiveness, as this of forgiveness is higher than that of revenge; but the philosophy of the will must be first understood.

With regard to forgiveness in the Creator, the theory is no more intelligible. 'God cannot forgive' is true, and it is curious how people lay hold of a little bit of a truth. *God cannot forgive;* His laws have assigned consequents entirely definite to every antecedent. Do we pray that he will prevent oxygen from uniting with hydrogen in the proportion of eight to one [*sic*] to form water? Neither can we pray that he will alter the laws of perfect goodness and wisdom with regard to spiritual things. *He* would not be perfect goodness and wisdom if He did. But the theory of forgiveness, as the Anglican Church holds it, is besides, a confused one. What sign have we that we are forgiven? How do we know when we are forgiven? The Roman Catholic is more sensible, who takes his beads and says so many paternosters for every sin, as his confessor orders. 'We don't know how to pray,' he says, 'therefore we take our Saviour's form of prayer, which is much better than anything we can say, and we take each sin in succession, and say, "Forgive us our trespasses," etc.; and then say, "that sin is forgiven, now on to the next."' Is not this the theory of the rosary when used 'in union with' our Saviour's sufferings? The Roman Catholic does think of his sins enough to tell them each and individually to a priest, who is the intermediary, and who tells him whether he is sorry enough, and, if he is, gives him absolution, though what takes place when we are absolved we do not know. But Protestants have such a 'slovenly unhandsome' way of doing the business. We will not even take the trouble of enumerating our sins, but we say, in order to save ourselves that trouble, 'We have done those things which we ought not to have done,' in order to include everything; and then '*bang* comes the absolution', without more ado. But what takes place when we are forgiven? Is it a change in God or in man? What is it? We know no more than if you were speaking Chinese. ...

The doctrine of forgiveness, though an advance upon that of revenge, is still, therefore, the great mistake with regard to God's character, the character of the Perfect, of perfect wisdom and goodness.

The Spirit of Right could not forgive without an absurdity. Will God make that which has been, not to have been? alter that which is past? The prayer would be impertinent, if it were not absurd. For it is asking the Spirit of Right to produce a contradiction, to be in opposition to Himself. But He is always the same; 'yesterday, to-day, and forever.'

Remorse – an untrue feeling?

If the existence of universal law be granted, then *remorse* is not a true feeling – not a feeling of what really *is*; for remorse is blame to ourselves for the past. But if the origin of our will, and our will itself, were, as it has been in accordance with law, there cannot, in truth, be blame to ourselves, personally, individually.

A distinction should be made as clearly as possible between absence of blame in an individual to himself, where he is conscious that he has been wrong, and indifference to that wrong.

To a healthy moral nature, having on an occasion erred, it would be as impossible to be indifferent to that error, though he should believe that it had not been in his possibility to avoid it, as it would be to one who should receive a bodily wound to be indifferent because it was not his fault.

We object to saying that a man *could* not have willed otherwise than he did, because this sounds as if he would or might have willed otherwise, but was under a necessity imposed by other and external power. We mean that the conditions on which will depends were such that, law being what it is, it was not possible that other will than that which did exist should exist.

We are most anxious to show that such an understanding of law, as manifested in human will and act, does not lead to indifference to right or wrong, but the contrary.

For a man to give way to feelings of remorse – of blame for what it has not been in him to prevent – is *not* true. To be conscious that wrong is wrong – to hold it in repugnance as all that we have to fear or avoid in our life and being – *is* true.

The more our state of being is human, manly, in the proper sense of those words, [11] the greater will be our repugnance to what is morally wrong, till wilfully to do wrong shall become an impossibility. The mind will *accord* with right, which is God's thought or consciousness, or will thirst and long and strive to do so, not in fear of His anger, but in love of right – of God, the living

113

consciousness of right. Indifference to wrong is in the moral nature as blindness, paralysis in the physical nature, and would not follow as the consequence of believing that right is our health and weal; that it is conditional – that, if ignorant – if unable, either from want of will, of knowledge, or of power, to keep those conditions – we fall into our greatest, our only essential harm. Such a belief would lead to the pursuit of right, as including all man has to desire; to avoidance of wrong, as including all man has to avoid.

Our experience is, that to dwell on the past error with feelings of remorse depresses the energy, all of which is wanted to pursue the right in future.

When we are conscious of past mistake, whether it arose from ignorance of the right, or whether we had knowledge which might have directed us, but had not will, let us set ourselves at once with all vigour to the life, the work of the present. Let us look upon the past as not almost but altogether springing from the righteous law of God. Let us accept the suffering of our mistake, accept our present work. Let trust in the redeeming power of God's law to invigorate us. Let us not spare ourselves the full consciousness of our mistake, let us look at our error as far as it may help us to truth. Let us strengthen our consciousness that there is no good but in the true and the right. Let us work on, even through our own faults and mistakes, with a noble striving for accordance with God's universal work.

Away with regrets which have no true foundation, empty your heart of them! Work out the page of to-day with goodwill, even though the mistake of yesterday may have complicated it. That very mistake shall lead to a brighter page than could have been, but that God, while his everlasting law of right secures us from all lasting evil, and assures us of all lasting good, gives to *us* to work the divine out of the human, to transmute ignorance into knowledge and feeling of truth.

But shall we have motive to avoid error, if we cease to suffer the pangs of regret and remorse?

There is a higher, better, truer help than those pangs – you will never rise high goaded by them. Strive to awaken the divine spirit of love in yourself, to awaken it in doing your present work, however you may have erred in the past – this will help you far better than dwelling on your own mistakes. There is nothing elevating or animating in the dissection of *them*. Essentially, in their very nature, they bring suffering or privation. Bear it in a true spirit, and work on. Turn your mistakes to as much account as you can, for the gaining of experience, but, above all, work on, yield not to paralyzing, depressing retrospection. God gives us the noble privilege of working out His work. He does not work for us. He gives us the means to find the way we should go. An eternal course is before us.

The tyranny of family life
The family uses people, *not* for what they are, nor for what they are intended to be, but for what it wants them for – for its own uses. It thinks of them not as what God has made them, but as the something which *it* has arranged that they shall be. If it wants some one to sit in the drawing-room, *that* some one is to be supplied by the family, though that member may be destined for science, or for education, or for active superintendence by God, *i.e.*, by the gifts within.

This system dooms some minds to incurable infancy, others to silent misery.

And family boasts that it has performed its mission well, in as far as it has enabled the individual to say, 'I have *no* peculiar work, nothing but what the moment brings me, nothing that I cannot throw up at once at anybody's claim'; in as far, that is, as it has *destroyed* the individual life. And the individual thinks that a great victory has been accomplished, when, at last, she is able to say that she has 'no personal desires or plans'. What is this but throwing the gifts of God aside as worthless, and substituting for them those of the world?

The prison which is called a family, will its rules ever be relaxed, its doors ever be opened? What is it, especially to the woman? The man may escape, and does. The cases where a child inherits its parents' tastes are so rare that it has passed almost into a proverb. The son of a celebrated man is never a celebrated man: the two Herschels, [12] the two Mills, [13] are mentioned as memorable exceptions. A son scarcely ever adopts his father's profession, except when compelled, as in the case of caste; and in the countries where caste prevails, the race deteriorates. How often a parent is heard to say, 'All that I have done will go to rack and ruin when I am gone. I have none to come after me who will keep it up!' It is said that the chances are 200 to 1, where a man's immediate descendants consist of three children and three grandchildren, against there being found one among these six who inherits his tastes and pursuits.

The law of God, it seems, is *against* repetition. Whatever the family, whatever the similarity of education, circumstances, etc., repetition is never seen. And is

this extraordinary? In chemistry, the mixture of two substances constitutes an entirely new substance, of which
neither the colour nor any of the properties can be predi-
cated from a knowledge merely of the colour or any of
the properties of the two original substances. So, in the
family, though there can be traced, it is true, the family
character, the family likeness, yet the children are all strikingly unlike each parent, strikingly unlike each other.
Here the analogy with chemistry *appears* to cease, for the
product of two chemical substances is always the same,
under the same circumstances. But, such are the minute
differences of circumstances which we never estimate,
that the analogy may still remain; and, as it is said that
there are no two leaves alike upon the same tree, so, and
much more, there never were created two human beings
alike. Now, what do we do with these *un*likenesses? The
family strives to make them all do the same thing. If one
of the family, as often happens, is superior to the rest, the
rest, and especially the heads of the family, seem to want
this one to be one with them, as we try to be one with
God; he is to devote all his talent and genius to forward
their ideas, not to have any new ones; to put their opinions, their thoughts, and feelings into a better dress, a
more striking light, not to discover any new light; and,
above all, he is not to find out any untruth in their ideas,
or think he has any new truth, 'for there is no such thing!'

To help others by *living* – by being *oneself*, is not this
the true meaning of sympathy, the true benefit of companionship? But, in general, we have to live by *not* being
ourselves. And what a fatiguing way of life it is! When we
are not afraid of being ourselves, when we suit the people
we are with, when what we say and feel does not shock

them or annoy them or frighten them, life is easy, life is improving, we make progress. Now, *how* often does this happen in one's own family, where one can rarely speak without implying blame of something, without knocking against some one's prejudices? And can it be otherwise when people are chained up together for life, so close in the same cage? It is often said that you are less known by your own family than by any one else. Is it wonderful? There is much of which you can never venture to speak. 'The extra-ordinary reserve which he (or she) maintained with his (or her) own family' are words so common that every one has heard them, and yet they are always uttered as if it were a solitary, or, as it is put, an *extraordinary* fact. 'He is so much more agreeable out of his own family,' is another common remark. And how often you see 'his' countenance fall when he is speaking to one of his own kin! As long as the iron chain is drawn tight round the family, fettering those together who are not joined to one another by any sympathy or common pursuit, it must be so. It is often disputed what kinds of character like society. It is probable that those like it who can say aloud the things which they would think to themselves, if they were alone. But how few can do this at home! There is no tyranny like that of the family, for it extends over the thoughts.

Merely to protest against ordinary family life is of no use at all – will only shock people: you must show a better life.

We would not destroy the family, but make it larger. We would not prevent people from having ties of blood, but we would secure all that the family promises, by enlarging it.

Monasteries, according to their original plan, were a much larger circle than the family. For there people did meet for a common object: those who had a vocation for work went into a house which supplied their kind of work – for contemplation, into a house of contemplation. Afterwards they degenerated into places of idleness and vice. But, in their original idea, they were places where people who liked to work for the same object, met to do so; and the enormous rate at which they multiplied showed how they responded to a want in human nature. Each was employed according to his or her vocation; there was work for all; but there is no such possibility in the family.

We want to give that which the family *promises* to give and does not. We want to extend the family, not annihilate it. We want 'not to destroy, but to fulfil' the hopes it holds out to supply the sympathy, the love, the fellow-feeling, the tenderness which it offers to supply and does not. Where is there such rudeness as in a family? Every where but in our own family our feelings are regarded. Now, we want to make a family where there shall be companionship in work, mutual attraction, love, and tenderness, we want to make *God's* family. We would not take away *anything*, we would enlarge and multiply.

But where is there such absence of tenderness, such constant contention as in a family? and the oddest part of the thing is that everybody thinks it peculiar to themselves.

No, certainly, family does not answer its purpose (nor is it likely it should among five or six) – we want to make it do so.

*

'Robbed and murdered' we read in the newspapers. The crime is horrible. But there are people being robbed and murdered continually before our eyes, and no man sees it. 'Robbed' of all their time, if robbing means taking away that which you do not wish to part with, slowly 'murdered' by their families. There is scarcely any one who cannot, in his own experience, remember some instance where some amiable person has been slowly put to death at home, aye, and at an estimable and virtuous home.

With regard to time, however, it is often said that if people made the most of their odd moments, they would have not much to complain of – but they waste their spare quarters of an hour so grievously.

The maxim of doing things at 'odd moments' is a most dangerous one. Would not a painter spoil his picture by working at it 'at odd moments'? If it be a picture worth painting at all, and if he be a man of genius, he must have the whole of his picture in his head every time he touches it, and this requires great concentration, and this concentration cannot be obtained at 'odd moments', and if he works without it he will spoil his work. Can we fancy Michael Angelo running up and putting on a touch to his Sistine ceiling at 'odd moments'? If he did he would have to take it out again. But the value of fresco is that this cannot be done, and that is one reason probably why great masters preferred fresco, and said that oils were only fit 'for children and dogs'. The very gist of fresco painting is that it should be all painted in at once from one master idea, not niggled and dawdled at.

The Chancellor Oxenstiern [14] is recorded to have written a folio volume during the ten minutes his wife kept him waiting for dinner every day.

It was not worth his writing, then, nor our reading. Everything that has ever been done at 'odd moments' had better never have been done; even a letter, written in a 'spare quarter of an hour' had better not have been written. Can any work requiring thought be done at 'odd times'? Perhaps the mere writing what has been carefully thought out in the watches of the night – yet hardly even that, to any good.

Then are we to do nothing with our odd times? Are we to waste the spare moments which make up the greater portion of a woman's life? If you are to do *any-* thing, you must do it then, is again said.

When people give this advice, it sounds as if they said, 'Don't take any regular meals. But be very careful of your spare moments for eating. Be always to ready to run into the kitchen and snatch a slice of bread and butter at odd times. But never sit down to your dinner, you can't, you know.' We know what *can* be done at odd times, a little worsted work, acquiring a language, copying something, putting the room to rights, mending a hole in your glove. What else is there? I don't know. Nothing requiring original thought: nothing, it is evident, which requires a form, a completeness, a beginning and an end, a whole, which cannot be left off 'at any time' without injury to it, which is not 'mere copying', in short.

When Beethoven wrote a bar, he must have had the phrase, the movement, the quick time which was to succeed, the slow movement which came before – the whole piece, in short, in his thought. And could he write a bar now, a bar then, at an 'odd moment'? This is what we call being a 'dilettante', when a man does work in that way, and most of the works of Dilettanti had better not have been. Women are at most always dilettanti, and have women ever produced any original work, any, with a *very* few exceptions, which the world would not be as well without?

Many, indeed, are the stories told of great men mastering a whole science in their spare moments.

There are, no doubt, some minds which can work, and some employments which can be taken up at odd times – where it is *acquiring* which is to be done. But if there is no digesting done, or if there is no time for digesting afterwards, the acquiring perhaps is not of much benefit, or a mind may become so possessed with a subject that it can work at it at *all* moments, but then the moments cease to be 'odd'. The greater genius which cannot and ought not to work without seeing the whole of its subject before its eyes, the most important subjects of thought which require this, these cannot be referred to 'odd moments'. People get out of the difficulty by not having *any* subjects of thought, which require to be pursued at other than 'odd times'.

How, in a family, where the one has to wait for the other – where, if they have any amiability, the employments of every one are constantly called upon to give way – how can the members, excepting those who have professions, ever have anything but 'spare moments'?

How indeed? We constantly hear it said, 'So and so has given up all her music since she married, or her drawing – what a pity, such a first-rate artist as she was!' A married woman cannot follow up anything which requires exercise, and if, even for such second-rate things as these, people cannot command the time necessary, how will they do for subjects of *thought*? And we are slower still to apprehend that we must rob you of the state of mind *with* which to think, than of the time *in* which to think. If visitors come in, the lady of the house often complains that she will not have time to do this or that, she does not complain that she will not be in a state of mind when they go, to do it, if it is something important and requiring thought. She settles *that* by not having anything important to think about.

Half the people in the world have, indeed, no power of thinking. 'What does it matter to give me time for that which I cannot do?' is often said.

But 'half the world cannot think,' *because* they have never tried. How is it possible? People get up in the morning and come down to breakfast, can they think then? After that, they read the newspapers or write letters, or sit in a room reading a book, where everybody is reading bits out of their own book aloud, or talking, till luncheon. Then they ride or drive, then they read a book or write letters till dinner. Then they spend the evening together till bed-time. This is interspersed, for women, with housekeeping, and visiting the poor people; for men, the House of Commons, managing their estates, the bench, and the board. Now, how are you to think? When are you to think? Not sitting with your feet on the fender, that is only dreaming. Few, except Descartes, ever thought without a pen in their hands.

A mother will say to her daughter, 'Now, my dear, all the people are gone, you have all the afternoon to yourself, you can go up and employ yourself in your own room.' But is she in a state to think? Is not her power of attention all frittered away? If she has breakfasted in a crowd, if she has been standing about for two or three hours afterwards, not knowing whether she might go away or not, how is her mind in any condition to think after that time? Sir Walter Scott even did not write his novels in that way.

But we are not all Sir Walter Scotts, nor Michael Angelos, nor Beethovens. On the contrary, such geniuses only come once in a thousand years.

How do we know that? We are often struck by the richness of organizations at 17 or 18, and how they go off afterwards. We are oftener surprised by the power than by the poverty of young characters. In many families there is one with a great dramatic talent, another with a genius for music, and a third with one equally remarkable for the pencil; a fourth writes like Coleridge. Yet we know perfectly well that these will be neither Michael Angelos, nor Beethovens, nor Mrs Siddonses, [15] nor Miltons. Why? Mrs A. has the imagination, the poetry of a Murillo, [16] and has sufficient power of execution to show that she might have had a great deal more. Why is she not a Murillo? From a material difficulty, not a mental one. If she has a knife and fork in her hands during three hours of the day, she cannot have a pencil or brush. Dinner is the great sacred ceremony of this day, the great sacrament. To be absent from dinner is equivalent to being ill. Nothing else will excuse us from it. Bodily incapacity is the only apology valid.

A lady friend of mine and Michael Angelo both had a turn for architecture. Michael Angelo studied it. My friend never did. All she did was pure genius. To compare her with Michael Angelo, of course, does not come into our head for a moment. How could she be compared, indeed? The one had no possibility given her, the other had. But people never think of this. They think nothing of being in a *state of mind* to think a great thought, to do a great work. They will fritter away all their power; and then think they have enough to do anything *they* want to do with it. They will let others play with them all the morning, and then think, 'I shall have the afternoon to myself.' You may do your accounts, or you may play with the children, or you may read an idle book, but do anything important which requires thought you cannot. And therefore the best way is to give up all subjects of thought, and that is what people do.

A female saviour?

It seems as if the female spirit of the world were mourning everlastingly over blessings, *not* lost, but which she has never had, and which, in her discouragement, she feels that she never will have, they are so far off.

The more complete a woman's organization, the more she will feel it, till at last there shall arise a woman, who will resume, in her own soul, all the sufferings of her race, and that woman will be the Saviour of her race.

Jesus Christ raised women above the conditions of mere slaves, mere ministers to the passions of the man, raised them by his sympathy, to be ministers of God. He gave them moral activity. But the Age, the World, Humanity, must give them the means to exercise this moral activity, must give them intellectual cultivation, spheres of action.

Was Christ called a complainer against the world? Yet all these great teachers and preachers must have had a most deep and ingrained sense, a continual gnawing feeling of the miseries and wrongs of the world. Otherwise they would not have been impelled to devote life and death to redress them. Christ, Socrates, Howard, [17] they must have had no ear for the joys, compared to that which they had or the sorrows of the world.

They acted, however, and we complain. The great reformers of the world turn into the great misanthropists, if circumstances or organization do not permit them to act. Christ, if He had been a woman, might have been nothing but a great complainer. Peace be with the misanthropists! They have made a step in progress; the next will make them great philanthropists; they are divided but by a line.

The next Christ will perhaps be a female Christ. But do we see one woman who looks like a female Christ? or even like 'the messenger before' her 'face', to go before her and prepare the hearts and minds for her?

To this will be answered that half the inmates of Bedlam begin in this way, by fancying that they are 'the Christ.'

People talk about imitating Christ, and imitate Him in the little trifling formal things, such as washing the feet, saying his prayer, and so on; but if any one attempts the real imitation of Him, there are no bounds to the outcry with which the presumption of that person is condemned.

For instance, Christ was saying something to the people one day, which interested Him very much, and interested them very much; and Mary and his brothers came in the middle of it, and wanted to interrupt Him, and take Him home to dinner, very likely (how natural that story is! does it not speak more home than any historic evidences of the Gospel's reality?), and He, instead of being angry with their interruption of Him in such an important work for some trifling thing, answers, 'Who is my mother? and who are my brethren? Whosoever shall do the will of my Father which is in heaven, the same is my brother and sister and mother.' But if we were to say that, we should be accused of 'destroying the family tie', of 'diminishing the obligation of the home duties'.

He might as well say, 'Heaven and earth shall pass away, but my words shall not pass away.' His words will never pass away. If He had said, 'Tell them that I am engaged at this moment in something very important; that the instruction of the multitude ought to go before any personal ties; that I will remember to come when I have done,' no one would have been impressed by His words; but how striking is that, 'Behold my mother and my brethren!'

The character of Christ

But what a character his was! When he talks about the baptism and the fire he has to go through, how expressive those words are! A baptism of fire he might well have called it. Every person must be baptized with fire who would do anything which is not usually done in the conventional walk of his life, which is not provided for in the ordinary course of things. Every person must have a baptism of fire who is not satisfied with the world as it is, and who would fain help it out of its rut. 'And how am I straitened till it be accomplished!'

But there are many things he said, which are very beautiful, and yet are not true. When they brought the woman taken in adultery before him, and he turned aside and wrote in an absent mood on the ground, and then said, 'He that is without sin among you, let him first cast a stone at her' – that beautiful tender spirit felt truly. But still there is a right and a wrong about adultery. This would be putting an end to all law and justice. If no one is to execute the law unless he be perfectly pure himself, the Lord Chief Justice and the Chief Baron must vacate their seats on the bench, and the police be disbanded, and the criminal jurisprudence of a country come to an end.

And when he implied that we should take no more thought than the lilies of the field, is that absolute truth?

And what he tells the Samaritan woman of the 'living water' is very beautiful, but when she does not understand, he seems to make no effort to explain to her. He was so filled and absorbed with his own thought that he seems to have spoken absently, and hardly to have cared whether she understood or not. He even sometimes says, 'That seeing they may see, and not perceive, and hearing they may hear, and not understand.' Might not the people have said, if you are to teach us, would it not be better to speak so that we can understand?

What a point he seems to have made about faith, believing that we can do a thing! 'Faith can remove mountains.' Now, it is very true that very often we do not believe we can do a thing, which, if we did believe it, we could do. But we may believe we can do a thing which we can't. A great many, from ignorance of the laws of God, have done so. Believing does not make us able to do it; does not make the law of God by which to do it. He seems to have known the first fact, and to have confused the second with it.

But what have we made of Christ in these vulgar times? We have daubed him all over with bright colours, so that we can hardly see through to the original beautiful form underneath. The churches have made him a God, and said, What! do you think you are like Christ? while they are preaching you to imitate him. The Unitarians have made him a perfect man, preaching that of which you see a great deal is not true. If we could but show him in his original form! The idea of a divine being dying to save you from another being does excite some feeling; but to tell you to listen to preaching which is perfect, and which you see is imperfect, and the whole of which you *cannot* believe, excites no feeling at all. If he is to be merely a teacher or merely a God, he is nothing.

Christ was the most spiritual being who has ever lived. But surely he made mistakes. He is generally considered *either* as God or as an impostor. Now, much progress cannot be made unless we admit that he made mistakes, and we, Protestants, who profess to be the upholders of the Bible, do admit it practically, though we assert theoretically, that He was plenarily inspired, a man-God. What do boards of guardians make, for instance, of this his counsel of 'poverty'? Those who do not admit His wonderful spirituality cannot make much progress either. He was not a reasoner, certainly. For sometimes he speaks of leaving father and mother and lands as a sacrifice, and offers compensation elsewhere; and sometimes he tells us to hate them, and then it cannot be a sacrifice. He certainly was so indignant with the lukewarm spirit of the times, which was always making excuses, that he spoke in very strong words, 'Let the dead bury their dead,' 'Hate your father and your mother,' 'Who is my mother and my brethren?'

The truth of the matter is probably that the attraction between husband and wife, and between all other friends should be this, that those two can do the work of God better together than apart, and then there would be no occasion to 'leave them for His name's sake,' but the contrary. When you have taken a wife, and undertaken the responsibility of children, *without* any such attraction, certainly there is no right in leaving them. With regard to leaving brothers and sisters, and father and mother, you have undertaken no charge with regard to them, and these should be left anyhow for God's work.

The spiritual life
Unless you make a life which shall be the manifestation of your religion, it does not much signify what you believe.

Our religious creed consists in this – belief in an omnipotent eternal spirit of love, wisdom, righteousness, manifesting itself by calling into existence, by definite laws, beings capable of the happiness of love, wisdom, righteousness – capable of advancing themselves and each other in divine nature – living in an universe in which, by definite law, the means and inducement are afforded which insure their advance through their own activity to humanity's blessedness. ...
What do we mean by spirituality?
Is it not *feeling*, as distinct both from intellect and from the affection of one human being to another? We do not call love, admiration, reverence, for a human being, spirituality, nor the trust which one human being has in another. These we call humanizing influences; but feelings called forth by the consciousness of a presence of higher

nature than human, unconnected with the material, these we call spiritual influences; and this we are conscious is the highest capability of our nature. Whenever we love, admire, reverence, trust this higher presence – whenever we sympathize with, partake in the purpose, thought, feeling, of this highest presence – these are our best moments.

Sympathy with man, interest in any right or innocent object, is not excluded by this higher state, is never indeed perfectly right and healthy, except in connexion with it.

There *are* modes (all in accordance with law) of vivifying and strengthening spirituality.

Fasting and prayer are usually supposed to be these modes. All undue or inappropriate care for anything does indeed check spirituality. The saints discovered this, experimentally, no doubt. So they took to banishing agreeable food and cheerful converse, even where not wrong. Except in a few great instances (St Bernard, St Ignatius Loyola, St Vincent of Paul, etc.) [18] denying the flesh its due made it only cry out, instead of leaving the being free for highest things. But the wish, the seeking for spirituality, which inspired a few among the saints, was, perhaps, higher than anything now existing.

Many went to convents and hermitages, hoping to win heaven or ward off hell; many to be applauded or to gain in some way in this world; many thinking to do God service, or give Him pleasure by sacrificing themselves or worshipping Him. But there is evidence that a few sought a spiritual state of being as their object, which no Church, scarcely any individual, seeks now. Spiritualism is dormant, not dead, let us hope. How to revive it, to rekindle it into life, is the great question.

*

Of all the fatal mistakes that have been made to impede the progress of the human race, this perhaps has been the most fatal, viz., the superstition that we have nothing to do but to exert the will, as it is called, and all former error will be rectified, all future good secured. If this mistake had been made with regard to the physical health, mankind would probably have come to an end. If we believed that a man with one diseased lung has nothing to do but to will, in order to have two good ones; if we believed that a man when he is hungry has nothing to do but to will in order to eat, the human race would soon perish. Are not the laws of the spiritual world at least as numerous, important, and worthy of study as those of the physical?

To think that we can be good under *any* circumstances is like thinking that we may be healthy when we are living over a sewer. If a person has to go to an unhealthy climate, he does not say, 'I can be well if I choose under any climate,' but he takes means, as far as he can, to arrange other healthy circumstances. If the heat is intense, he takes care to have exercise in the early morning; if the dews are hurtful, he takes care not to be out just at sunset; so there may be circumstances under which a man cannot be good and yet which he cannot, at present, rightly alter. In that case it is not by saying, 'I can be good, if I only will, under any circumstances,' that he will maintain himself so; but by supplying, as much as in him lies, circumstances which will make him so.

Here, again, comes in that fatal mistake about the will. The boy William is good and happy in some occupation for which he has a vocation, that is, to which God calls him. If it is right for the convenience of parents or for the conventional code that he should adopt some other occupation, parents seldom hesitate to say, 'This is not the thing for you, go and be good and happy in the Law, or the Church, or at College'; and they would not doubt but that it was in his power to say, 'I *will* go and be good and happy in the Law, or in the Church, or at College.' To *say* it is, indeed, in his power, and, if he is amiable and feeling, he will probably try to say it; but to *be* it may not BE in his power; and this is just the practical mistake which shows the want of a true conception about the will. It is taken for granted that there is this uncomprehended something, called 'will', which what we call 'William' can command, what we call 'will' will obey, without our understanding what man is, what the man William is, what the will is; and thus among well-intentioned people, half the mischief in life arises. What a dangerous immoral doctrine, people say, that we are in the hands of circumstances. No, we are in the hands of God.

'I can be good if I will' is the road to despair; for a person says, 'I will be good when I go back to such and such circumstances; I resolve to be good; I know I can if I will.' He 'wearies Heaven with prayer'; he fails and falls; he thinks the fault lies in his will, and he sinks lower and lower till he gives himself up as lost.

But we don't *only* say 'will'! There are 'means appointed' for our 'growth in grace'.

Observance of the Sabbath

'To-morrow is Sunday!' and what a curious thought that to-morrow, in all the length and breadth of Christendom, people will put on their best clothes, and be in time for church, and think that they have performed a duty by going to church, and hardly anybody will really feel anything whatever, when there.

And what is the cause of its being Sunday to-morrow all over the Christian world? Why is Sunday kept?

From the feeling of a Superior Being.

But why does that make people put on their best clothes?

Out of a feeling of respect to Him.

But we appear to think this Superior Being more particular about the fashions than about the arts, for there is such singing in the church as you would not suffer for a moment in your drawing-room. Such reading aloud there is as you would not allow in your own family; nowhere is such reading as the clerk's ever heard, except in church. 'Let us sing to the honour and glory of God,' and then such music follows as is certainly not to the honour and glory of the singers. Then, although the people are dressed in their best, the church is not; it is generally so uncomfortable, ugly, and bare a place that you would not go into it, if it were not the house of God. God's house is much dirtier and shabbier than anybody else's house. We feel so strongly the necessity of a Sabbath – a day of rest – a day peculiarly devoted to religious thought and feeling and to their expression by God's children gathered to-gether, that surely, whatever external aid is called in from art, as music, architecture, etc., should be of the best.

One day in seven set apart by common consent of all the world for finding out the spiritual laws of God is indeed an inestimable advantage. We should like to have two. ...

Worship

As to a 'common worship' as it is called, instead of having it once a week, we would have it every day, twice a day. The word *'worship'*, however, seems hardly to express what God wants of us. He does not want to be praised, to be adored, to have his glory sung. We can scarcely conceive a good man, a very limited edition of God's perfections, wishing it. How inappropriate, then, to Him all this praise! And many only give it, because they are afraid of Him, for how can He be really thought good, with such qualities as are ascribed to Him, vanity, anger, revenge.

What he desires seems to be accordance with Him, that we should be one with Him, not prostrate before Him.

'Submitting to God's will' is a phrase we cannot understand. It is as if you looked upon God as something apart, *without*, independent of all principle, to whom you have only to submit. But if, for 'God' we read 'the spirit of perfect love and wisdom', how can we talk about *submitting* to perfect love, directed by wisdom? We accord with it; we don't submit. It is often said, 'So-and-so is so good, she submits entirely to God' as a *merit*. In so far as she is good, she is part of the divine goodness, accordant with it, willing the same things, omnipotent in as far as she wills the same things. Is it not a mistake to call this submission? It is *oneness*. Christ's will was God's will – the will of love.

I would try to teach a child – not to 'submit' to God, nor to pray that anything should be otherwise – but to second Him. I would try to inspire it with the idea that it, the child, can second GOD!

Bible

What is morality to be referred to? Is it not to our sense of right? But we have referred it to a book, which book makes many contradictory assertions. Discoveries are being made every day in physical science; but in the most important science of all no discoveries are made or can be made. Why? because the book is final. Supposing Moses had written a book about mechanics, and this book was regarded as the ultimatum, we should have made no progress in mechanics. Aristotle was supposed to have written such a book, and for 1,800 years people disbelieved their own actual experience before their eyes, because they could quote chapter and verse of Aristotle to a contrary effect. Yes, with the sound of two weights falling simultaneously in their ears, they maintained that the weight which was ten times heavier than the other fell in one-tenth of the time of the other, because *Aristotle had said so*. Is not this an exactly parallel case?

Religion under this view, it will be said, will consist partly of assertions considered to be proved, partly of subjects for further consideration among mankind. Much is to be learnt from the Bible, and probably from all books which have been accepted by large portions of mankind as inspired; but man's capabilities of observation, thought, and feeling exercised on the universe, past, present, and to come, are the source of religious knowledge.

Prayer

It did strike me as odd, sometimes, that we should pray to be delivered 'from plague, pestilence, and famine', when all the common sewers ran into the Thames, and fevers haunted undrained land, and the districts which cholera would visit could be pointed out. I thought that cholera came that we might remove these causes, not pray that God would remove the cholera.

I gave up praying, in the sense of *asking*, from experience, and not from theory.

Observing whether prayer was answered, and finding it was not, it occurred to me that this was not God's plan, that His scheme for us was not that He should give us what we asked for, but that mankind should obtain it for mankind; that we were not paupers asking at a Poor Law Board for relief, but men working for themselves and their fellow-creatures.

It will be said, if we are to have no prayer, we lose our chief support and comfort in this painful world.

But what is the intercourse we now have with God? Prayer, in its present sense, is to give utterance, at stated times, to a form of flattery and to selfish or unwise requests. It is, as in the Litany, to say to God, 'Don't go this way, don't go that way,' till we have marked out the whole line which He ought to go, and interdicted to Him the fulfilling of almost every law which He has made.

We want, it is said, the direct personal communication with God and Christ, that we may ask and hear them answer. Do not take from us, is the cry, our Saviour, the Christ who died upon the cross for us.

And does not God do much more than die upon the cross for us? Is He not in every one of us, going through sin and suffering, 'descending into hell' with us? Does he not suffer, not once for us, but every day in us? And can we want anything more than communion with the perfect and eternal Father?

I want, it is said, communion with Christ, my divine brother, who feels for me.

And you will have it with the Son, the divine in man, with many Christs, who suffer for all mankind.

But we want a Son 'to make intercession for us.'

Do you suppose that Christ is ever 'making intercession' for us? It is true He 'ever liveth,' to work for us, but – to 'intercede' for us? He had better not exist at all, God had better not exist at all, than be employed in this way; the one in persuading, the other in being persuaded.

But we want an answer. It is no comfort to say that God may hear me, but He does not speak to me. Man wants an answer.

Can he receive it from the Eternal when he cannot comprehend what eternity is – from the Infinite and Perfect, when infinity and perfection are beyond His understanding? Were God to speak to him, could he hear? Were God to tell him His plans, could he comprehend them?

But God does not refuse to answer the longing, devoted spirit, which says, Speak, Lord, for thy loving child heareth. He hears as the Father; He answers as the Son, and as the Holy Spirit. I could not understand God, if He were to speak to me. But the Holy Spirit, the Divine in me, tells me what I am to do. I am conscious of a voice that I can hear, telling me more truth and good than I *am*. As I rise to *be* more truly and more rightly, this voice is ever beyond and above me, calling to more and more good.

But you have to invent what it says.

We believe that each man has his Holy Ghost; that is, the best part of himself inspired by God. But whether it is I who speak, or whether it is God speaking to me, I do not know. We call upon our fellow-creatures to study this subject. That Prayer, as *asking*, will entirely cease, we are certain. If we give up *asking, confessing* our sins and formal *praising*, will it be said, what remains to be expressed to God? Surely, infinite are the sympathies, infinite the thoughts and feelings, of man towards the Perfect Spirit, with whom he desires to be one.

Let us think what we should ask God to communicate, if we believed He would hear us, and grant what we ask.

Of that which is asked every day much is impossibility, because to grant it would be a contradiction to truth and wisdom. Much that we ask we shall certainly receive, because it is accordant with truth and wisdom that we should receive it; but is *asking* the true intercourse to hold with the Perfect, who is always telling, always offering all things?

We will *ask*, then, nothing of God. How ungracious, how stupid it is to ask the Gracious, the rich Giver, the wise Father, who is always offering all. But we will seek continually (and stimulate mankind to seek with us) to prepare the eye and ear of the great human existence, that seeing it *shall* perceive, and hearing it *shall* understand. 'Seek and ye shall find' – seek *wisely* must be added – 'knock, and it shall be opened' – knock, *i.e.*, not against a stone wall made to remain a wall, but at a door made to open. ...

Ask of perfect wisdom, you will have an answer above and beyond yourself. Speak, articulately or inarticulately, to perfect goodness and love, such existence hears you, answers you, through the exercise of your own nature, it is true, but it is not your own nature which answers you, but a higher. It is not the mere fact of using words which brings this answer. Many, many are the words spoken to this Holy Spirit which receive no response. Time has already disclosed conditions which, if kept, allow a communication between the holy spirit of God and the holy spirit in man. It used to be thought that God spoke occasionally to individuals, with no other condition than that it was His arbitrary will so occasionally to speak – that He called man out of his sleep with no reference to any particular state in man, the consequence of which would be always communication of the divine in man with God.

But experience shows that there are times when man may ask this communication, but cannot have it, because the conditions for having it have not been kept. But let him have patience to find out and to keep these conditions, and wisdom, and love and goodness, which he will feel above his own, will dwell with him; he may interpret their words.

Evidence for this may be found in experience. We believe, from experience, that man is capable of living always, as it were, in a state of reference to that higher Being – that, as the world's ways improve, far as we are from it now, man's intercourse with man will be regulated so as to help this higher intercourse, to keep it unbroken, whereas now it is almost impossible not to break it as soon as man is with his kind.

Deep souls who wanted it fled to wildernesses, to monasteries, and as always happens, others who did not comprehend them, imitated them, and fleeing from the world became a fashion; although it is hard to understand what it means, since the world is what we have to mould, not to fly from.

It is said that mysticism is mistaken in urging man to isolate himself with God, and devote himself exclusively to his Creator; whereas man's natural inclination, implanted in him by God, urges him to devote himself to his fellow-man, urges all mankind mutually to unite in benevolent ties. But those who say this do not see that the first motive for mankind to unite is devotion to God; that devotion to God is the spring of love to man, makes it necessary, is the same thing. One with God, one with man.

Why both humility and pride should be avoided

The parish clerk who said, 'You may pray for rain, but it's no use while the wind is in that quarter,' spoke according to experience and observation. In the same way we may pray for self-forgetfulness, but 'it's no use' while the wind is blowing from the quarter of luxury and idleness. We may pray for humility, but 'it's no use' while there is no wind of sufficient strength to blow our thoughts away from ourselves.

How many have struggled against a sin of vanity, and prayed and prayed, and gone through years of self-mortification, and self-inflicted tortures, and wondered why God was so far off, and whether 'His arm was shortened that He could not save' and why He was so deaf that He would not hear, and have been brought to the very verge of despair; 'the sorrows of death compassed me, and the pains of hell gat hold upon me;' whereas if they had lived a life which had afforded them one interest so strong as to make them forget themselves, they would have forgotten their own puny reputation from the mere force of another interest.

In the same way with pride. The desire to be something, to do something, is implanted in us. Everybody ought to command. No one's faculties are fully called out till they do command. There is nothing so invigorating, so inspiring, so regenerating. Everybody ought to obey. How delightful it is to obey some one who really knows what he is about, and can teach you – to learn, when one really feels that one is learning something. But let children speak and say how much they have learnt from their masters and their lessons.

Everybody ought, then, to command and to obey; and then we should hear no more of pride, and thinking much of oneself; for pride is the perversion of that desire of action which would then have found its proper exercise.

Great harm is done by striving after what is called 'humility', by checking what is called 'pride'. It is a cry of nature to wish to be some thing – to do something. To check it is to check the appetite for activity which God has placed in our nature.

Humility is thinking meanly of ourselves, placing ourselves below others, and being willing that others should do so too.

Is not this rather absurdity and untruth? What I want is a true estimate of myself, not a false one. I want to see myself as God sees me. If a man with great physical strength were to say to one who has none, you are stronger than I, you can cut down that tree better than I: we should say 'how wrong!' If Macaulay [19] were to persuade himself (for the sake of being humble) that he could not write history so well as any of the people at that moment walking down the Strand, would that be true or desirable? The maxim, let a man know what he can do, and do it, is not compatible with that of humility. Humility, if logically carried into our conduct, would lead to our giving up everything we do into the hands of those whom we are to strive to think can do it better than ourselves.

'Renouncing the world' would mean renouncing the great majority of mankind, of our fellow-men. Now mankind (or the world) is what we have to work upon. That we ought to seek the offices which we dislike most has no truth in it. Those who have an attraction, a fitness (and these are many) for cooking and sweeping, ought to be sent to do it, not those who have a dislike to it. To 'forget themselves and to despise the praises of men,' the Catholics say. But the way to 'forget yourself' (which is certainly of the first importance) is to be so much interested in some object out of yourself, that you can't remember yourself. If you are fully occupied, all your faculties in full and interesting exercise, you won't think about the praise of men.

Pride and conceit are not qualities either which will contribute to our oneness with God. But pride and conceit become impossible when we have a knowledge of the laws of God. If his laws have made me what I am, if without them I could not be what I am, and with them cannot be than what I am, how can I possibly be proud of what I am? They do away equally with pride and humiliation. The laws of God have brought me where I am. His laws will carry me through.

In 'mortifying' ourselves to gain blessedness, in 'humbling ourselves that we may be exalted' (though this is certainly founded on the words of Christ), there is a good deal of the spirit of doing things for the sake of reward, and this, of course, is untrue and unhealthy.

There may be a pride even in humility, a self-seeking in suffering 'abjection' (all pride is the effect of a narrowness of view), and therefore it is far safer not to be thinking about ourselves than to be seeking for 'mortification'. Besides, it is ungrateful to God, when He is seeking to give you pleasure, always to take the worst – *not that some one else may have the best*, but only for the sake of mortifying your*self* and especially, if you do this for the sake of having the best in another world.

To 'renounce worldly enjoyment' implies a mistake. It should *be* our enjoyment to do the world's work.

It does not improve us to 'hate' anything. One might easily excite oneself to hate all these luxuries. But it does us no good.

The Catholics say that 'through love of Christ's poverty the religious man should be glad when he has the poorest and worst things.'

Surely it is a mistake to recommend poverty. Surely it is a higher pursuit to have property, in order that we may devote it to Him and do His work with. ...

Men seem to think it will be pleasing to God that they should be ashamed of their human nature – they do not express sorrow that, endowed with a nature which has divine possibilities, they remain so poor: they prostrate themselves before the Source of all we are and all we might be, deploring their sinful nature – their impossibility to be or do anything that is right, except in as far as God works in and for them; and this is supposed to be humility pleasing to God. A just and true appreciation of what we are and what we may become, of how God will help us if we take the appointed means to receive His help, what He will do for us and what we are to do for ourselves, is the state which is true to our nature, true to God's nature. Pride is an aberration of mind, impossible except from misunderstanding of what we are, why we are, what we are to become. Self-satisfaction in humbling ourselves before God is misunderstanding as great in another direction. We can neither feel proud nor humble except from some misconception of God or of ourselves. If our state of mind is right, we shall press ever onward to be and to do in the infinite career before us. Such progress will be the want, the thirst of our nature – not undertaken to satisfy pride, not calling forth pride. To God we shall refer what we are, what we shall become, our means of becoming what it is fitting we should be. There will be no place in us where pride can enter. While the infinite is beyond, how can we feel proud of any step towards it?

The problems of religious communities

Religious *life* and work require the healthy state and devotion of the spiritual, the affectional, the intellectual, and the physical nature. Each community of men should modify itself, and choose its chief leader and all subordinate leaders with a view to rendering its life and its work in accordance with the Spirit whence springs life.

We should aim at implicit obedience to leadership, together with scope for individual exercise of idiosyncrasy – this is a difficult problem. ...

In practice, all religious orders, both Protestant and Roman Catholic, fail in this. Each generally consists of one powerful mind at the head, and a great many childish minds under him (or her). If by chance another powerful mind creeps in among the subordinates, it throws all into confusion, it is called and *is* troublesome, and it ends by being expelled, expelling, or becoming stupefied.

In practice, religious orders never make progress. Great minds found them; little minds spring out of them. There is scarcely a historical instance of a discoverer, an inventor, a genius, or a benefactor of mankind being produced by a religious order *after* it is once compact and established. This is easily accounted for. There exists a certain personality, a want of interest in mankind *in general*, in the efforts of others – a narrowness which leads the superior, who is (in theory and in reality) the moving spring, to think that his (still more her) own way is the only one for the world's salvation; that whatever does not spring from the same centre of thought is ruinous, and therefore to be discouraged; that the world, in fact, consists of himself (or herself), his (or her) community, and the poor immediately under their charge. There exists an impatience of interference (*all* other work being called by them 'interference' with their own). This makes the usefulness of 'orders' *per se* so narrow as to be nearly nugatory. I speak from experience. But the remark applies solely to those 'orders' and 'societies' which are not in constant official and essential contact with secular institutions. I speak quite as much of Protestant as of Roman Catholic 'societies'. The travelling 'Sisters of Charity' [20] are perhaps the least stereotyped, the most exempt from this *exclusiveness*, which, where it exists, destroys all progress. The true 'papacy', the real doctrine of 'infallibility', exists in its completeness only in the *self*-constituted unchecked head of an 'order', 'society', parish, congregation, or doctrine.

Yet, while anxious to avoid the evils which experience has shown to arise in religious orders, we yet believe that *associations* with the object of discovering truth concerning the nature and will of God, the duty and nature of man – how to regulate life in accordance with such truth – are the probable, the natural means for causing mankind to advance in true belief, in true life. If two or three, or if one only, finds contradictions to the truth within him in the taught beliefs and in the ordinary lives of mankind, we would say to the few or the one, 'Try to gain some few who would fervently wish to live *as one with God.*' But, if this is to be our endeavor, we must strive to know, and to declare to those few, the Being with whom we seek to be one. And here we may well imitate the best of the Roman Catholic orders, while on our guard against the evil incident to them. As with them, a fervently felt religion must be our bond. And, like the Roman Catholic orders, those who unite to seek a life springing from religion must unite in the reception of the same truth. We seek not to burn those who praise and worship, in God, what they would despise in man. We sympathize with parts of most religions. But if we unite together with a few to strive to live a life dictated by the Spirit of God, we must agree as to what that Spirit *is*. If *one* thinks it right to pray continually for forgiveness of sins, while another feels those sins to have been the cross which man bears for mankind, and that it is truth magnanimously to bear the cross of our past sins, while striving by God's means to emancipate ourselves and others from the burden of that cross – can these two be harmoniously, in life and feeling, one with God.

Is there an after-life?

Whence does the question arise, whether human consciousness will be continued after the existence of man, such as he is in this world? The plant withers and dies: we never think of asking whether there will be any continuation of its individuality; we are satisfied with observing that matter never ceases to exist, but only changes from one mode of existence to another. Of this the senses assure all who attend to the subject.

But very many are not satisfied to take it for granted that, when man dies, the change in his material form is the only result. The heart which has loved and sympathized, revered and admired, asks, 'Is this dust all that remains from qualities of the same nature as those to be recognized in the Perfect?' The heart which has watched suffering asks, when in vain trying to relieve it, 'Is there no relief but unconsciousness?' Still more, the heart which mourns over a vicious existence, conscious that, if this be all, for this man it would be better that he had never been born, since his existence is not worth having; yet, conscious also that he had no power to make it otherwise, asks whether there may not be future opportunity in which the experience of the past may lead to a better future? The capabilities of the nature of the plant are fulfilled; but man, to whose capabilities none can put a limit in themselves – man, full of high object, making discoveries, or otherwise exercising his faculties, so that his life is enriching mankind! Is he to share the fate of the plant?

But he bequeaths, it is said, the riches of his nature to posterity, when he himself becomes insensible dust.

Each individual is an idiosyncratic nature, different from every other that is, or has been or ever will be. It is impossible that he should communicate all that he is, all that he has to communicate, except through himself. Whatever the possibilities of his nature, it is by *exercise* only that he can realize or communicate them. To his power of attainment or of communication it does not seem that there is any necessary close before death. Many live to old age, in healthy possession of their faculties till death. That many do not, is owing to mistakes in the mode of life. The affection which any one feels to another, whose life he has shared, can never be repeated by any other. Fresh affections may arise between individuals of fresh generations. But can succession equal, in kind or degree, continuity? During the space of a brief human life, what is there not to do? There is to prepare the nature for such attachments, to find out, by the experience of actual life, the persons capable of being mutually inspired with them; there are the mistakes to be made; each other's characters to be felt after in the dark; and heart-aches from having misunderstood, or not adapted ourselves to the characters we are attached to.

But, granting that, each generation transmitting its experience, man will arrive at exemption from such mistakes; that, by dint of this experience transmitted by one generation to another, he will attain to a well-constituted nature, to good means of cultivating and exercising it, to a good organization of life, so that the most will be made of life, and thus that opportunity will not be lost by mistakes.

But then still more will it be felt that the ties of sympathy, of capability of communicating mutually, between any two, are different from what can be between any other two – that to put an end to such ties would be to destroy that which, by the laws of God, can never be again. Such destruction of that which is valuable – of that which can never be renewed, would not be consistent with the existence of an omnipresent spirit of love and wisdom.

Perhaps increased knowledge of the nature of God may reveal to us that each present mode of being is part of a development from a past without beginning, towards a future without end; all *except* the one eternal Spirit, whose thought, whose feeling, whose purpose, whose will, comprehends every other mode of being. ...

And if the thought, the sentiment of right, and love, and wisdom is eternal, will not its manifestation in life, in activity, be eternal?

And will this manifestation be an eternal development or an eternal succession? Development carries the past into the future; succession begins where the past has left off. The smallest seed which develops into a plant, carries on into that plant the nature of every seed which preceded it. The elective king or ruler takes up circumstances where his predecessor laid them down. In him is not development. The thought, the feeling, the character of man, is by far the most interesting mode of existence of which we have any knowledge or conception, except the thought, the feeling, the character of God.

Development from one individual thought, feeling, character to another, cannot take place by succession, by one character taking up circumstances where another left them.

Hence, perceiving development to be God's mode of proceeding, we are led to expect development from one state of character into another. ...

Is it asked, what beings will live after his life ceases?

Every mode of being which admits of thought and feeling; for such modes of being require eternity for their development. No thought, no feeling, can have attained perfection, can have acted and lived perfection, in any limited period. Each individual thinking, feeling being, by the law of the Perfect, works upward, directly or indirectly – attains to the perfect thought and feeling which comprehends all, which feels and wills all truth – and then again sets forth to work and live, and manifest, and realize fresh phases of being, guided by the law of the all-comprehensive spirit.

Now every present influences the character as an individuality. May we believe that each character is, and will remain, an individuality through eternity? Or must we suppose that the individuality goes on till, by progress, worked out by exercise, all knowledge is attained – till God's thought, which is the revelation of knowledge present, past, and future, is attained – and then His being is shared, His purpose is shared, viz., that of turning a fresh phase of purpose into life, exercise, work? But, then, will this bring to an end individual affections? Not necessarily; for the Perfect thus contains in His nature all the individual affections which ever were, matured by life and work, in one. And this one, in again individualizing, according to the laws of righteousness and benevolence, contains in its nature those same individuals which may again meet as individuals, again merge into perfection – perfection of thought and feeling, now and for ever, but such thought and feeling ever anew worked out in successive phases of life.

This is not pantheism, which asserts that man will be merged in God and lose his individuality.

'The spirit returns to God who gave it' *is* pantheism. And this cannot be true in the sense that it ceases to have a separate existence. Why, in that case, its trials? Can we suppose that God sent forth a being to suffer and struggle, merely in order that it should be re-absorbed into God's existence. Most lame and impotent conclusion. Why send it forth? To what end its suffering?

Individuality appears to be sacred in the thought of God. Indeed, if we suppose man to be a modification of the attributes of God limited by the laws of physical nature, it seems natural to expect that individuality will be preserved in every instance till perfection is attained.

Our real, practical reason for believing in a future life is the same that men believe upon and act upon throughout their practical life, viz. that *will* will correspond with the nature of the character whence it springs, and that that nature exists in accordance with some law or principle. Why do I depend on finding my meal prepared this morning? on meeting my friend at noon? on finding the committee collected which I expect this afternoon? Is it not all dependence upon will, upon the nature whence will springs? I find it to be essential to will to pursue its greatest satisfaction, or, in other words, I find that, essentially, it does not *dis*-satisfy itself. I can give no mathematical proof that, at nine o'clock, I shall find breakfast on the table – at three I shall find collected a committee for a particular purpose. But I no more doubt it than I doubt the existence of the pen and ink which I see before me.

Once assured that there exists a *will*, whence spring the successive phenomena or modes of existence in the universe; once convinced that the nature of that will is the same benevolence and wisdom of which I am conscious in human nature – and I depend on a continuation of existence. Because the Omnipotent willing otherwise would contradict the benevolence and wisdom which His universe reveals.

If you will strive to observe, study and comprehensively interpret the universe in its eternal purport, you will discern more and more one will, one nature, upon which you may depend. You could not bring yourself to conceive that your friends in this house would leave you this morning without your daily meal. Stretch your thought to the revelations of the universe, and still less will you feel it a possibility that God will quench the spirit than that man will starve the body.

The more, in ages to come, mankind shall become convinced, by the evil actually remedied by man, of human possibility to remedy all evil – of human possibility to progress in righteousness and knowledge by progress actually made – the more the experience how each existing character can help the human family as no other can – the stronger will become the conviction that each individuality is intended to help God's family in the universe after, as well as during, his present phase of being. Hence, without increased means of conceiving the mode of existence after death, human belief in it may be strengthened.

The ceaseless change which goes on through all existence except One, whose will directs it, is all development – all the fulfilling of purpose. Time, in one sense, is as nothing to the eternal One. He will realize the full, the perfect development which is His thought, though it require ages beyond the grasp of our minds to conceive.

Notes

[1]   Nightingale saw the God of the Spanish mystic, St Teresa of Avila, as capricious rather than lawful. But she was deeply interested in Teresa's writings.

[2]   Cf. Matthew 3.3: 'the voice of one crying in the *wilderness*'.

[3]   'Honour your father and your mother, that your days may be long in the land which the Lord your God gives you' (Exodus 20.12).

[4]   John Wesley (1703–91), founder of Methodism.

[5]   The word 'religion' possibly comes from the Latin *religare*, 'to bind'.

[6]   Nightingale saved many lives in the Crimea by her foresight in obtaining provisions.

[7]   John Dalton (1766–1844), English chemist and physicist, developed modern atomic theory.

[8]   In fact, Islam was originally founded without any miracles by Mahomet.

[9]   Dr Andrew Smith (1797–1872), Director-General of the Army Medical Department in 1853–8. During the Crimean War he was much criticized by the press and by Nightingale herself.

[10] Florence Nightingale wrote: 'In the Lord's Prayer, beautiful as it is, there is hardly a word of exact truth. "Our Father which art in heaven." If He is anywhere, He is *everywhere* – not more in heaven

than on earth. "Thy will be done in earth as it is in heaven." We do not know whether there is any other place where His will is done more than in this, at present; and, in one sense, His will is always done. "Forgive us our trespasses", when the trespasser is His pioneer, cannot be true. Neither can "deliver us from evil", when He made the evil by His laws on purpose to save us.' [Editors' note: the prayer to 'be kept this day from all sin' is from the Book of Common Prayer.]

[11] The Sanskrit root word *manas*, 'to think'.

[12] The astronomers William Herschel (1738–1822) and his son John Frederick William Herschel (1792–1871).

[13] John Stuart Mill and his father James Mill (1733–1836).

[14] Axel Oxenstiern (1583–1654), Chancellor of Sweden (1612–54), diplomat and administrative reformer during the Thirty Years War.

[15] Sarah Kemble Siddons (1755–1831), English actress.

[16] Bartolomé Estéban Murillo (161x–82), Spanish religious artist.

[17] Probably John Howard (1726–90), English philanthropist and reformer in the fields of public health and prison management.

[18] Bernard of Clairvaux (1090?–1153), French Cistercian mystic and Doctor of the Church. Ignatius of Loyola (1491–1556), Spanish spiritual director and founder of the Jesuit order. Vincent de Paul (1581–1660), founder of the Vincentian Congregation and of the Daughters of Charity.

[19] Thomas Babbington Macaulay (1800–1859),

English historian, essayist and statesman, and celebrated author of *The History of England* (5 vols., 1849–61).

[20] More properly, the Daughters of Charity of Saint Vincent de Paul. The order was founded in France in 1633 by St Vincent de Paul and St Louise de Marillac, and was devoted to caring for the sick and the poor.

Select Bibliography

Biographies

Allen, Donald R., 'Florence Nightingale: Towards a Psychohistorical Interpretation', *Journal of Interdisciplinary History* 6, 1 (Summer 1975), 23–45.

Cook, Sir Edward Tyas, *The Life of Florence Nightingale*, 2 vols., London: Macmillan, 1914.

Huxley, Elspeth, *Florence Nightingale*. New York: G. P. Putnam's Sons, 1975.

Smith, F. B., *Florence Nightingale, Reputation and Power*. London: Croom Helm, 1982.

Strachey, Lytton, *Eminent Victorians*. London: Chatto and Windus, 1918.

Woodham-Smith, Cecil Blanche, *Florence Nightingale 1820–1910*. London: Constable, 1950.

Letters

Vicinus, Martha, and Nergaard, Bea, eds., *Ever Yours, Florence Nightingale*. London: Virago, 1989.

Goldie, Sue M., *'I have done my duty': Florence Nightingale in the Crimean War, 1854–56*. Manchester University Press, 1987.

Texts

Calabria, Michael D., and Macrae, Janet A. (eds.), *Suggestions for Thought: selections and commentaries*. University of Pennsylvania Press, 1994.

Nightingale, Florence, *Letters from Egypt*. A. and G. A. Spottiswoode, 1854.

Nightingale, Florence, *Letters from Egypt: A Journey on the Nile, 1849–1850*. Selected and with an introduction by Anthony Sattin. London: Weidenfeld and Nicholson, 1987.

Nightingale, Florence, 'A "Note" of Interrogation', *Fraser's Magazine*, 87, n.s. 7 (May 1873), 567–77 (available in the British Library).

Nightingale, Florence, *Notes on Nursing; what it is and what it is not*. New York: Dover Publications, 1969.

Nightingale, Florence, *Notes on Matters Affecting the Health, Efficiency and Hospital Administration of the British Army*. Harrison and Sons, 1858.

Nightingale, Florence, 'A Sub-"Note of Interrogation"', *Fraser's Magazine*, 88, n.s. 8 (July 1873), 25–36 (available in the British Library).